Solving
genealogy problems

Other titles for genealogists from How To Books

YOUR FAMILY TREE ON-LINE
How to trace your ancestry from your own computer
Dr Graeme Davis

RESEARCH YOUR SURNAME
and your family tree
Dr Graeme Davis

HOW TO TRACE YOUR IRISH ANCESTORS
*An essential guide to researching and documenting
the family histories of Ireland's people*
Ian Maxwell

WRITE YOUR LIFE STORY
*How to organise and record your memories
for family and friends to enjoy*
Micheal Oke

Write or phone for a catalogue to:

How To Books
Spring Hill House
Spring hill Road
Begbroke
Oxford
OX5 1RX
Tel. 01865 375794

Or email: info@howtobooks.co.uk

Vist our website www.howtobooks.co.uk
to find out more about us and our books

Like our Facebook page How To Books & Spring Hill

Follow us on Twitter @Howtobooksltd

Read our books online www.howto.co.uk

Solving
genealogy problems

How to break down 'brick walls'
and build your family tree

Dr Graeme Davis

howtobooks

Published by How To Books Ltd,
Spring Hill House, Spring Hill Road,
Begbroke, Oxford OX5 1RX
Tel: (01865) 375794. Fax: (01865) 379162
info@howtobooks.co.uk
www.howtobooks.co.uk

How To Books greatly reduce the carbon footprint of their books by sourcing their
typesetting and printing in the UK.

British Library Cataloguing in Publication Data
A catalogue record for this book is available from the British Library

ISBN: 978 1 84528 477 0

Cover design by Baseline Arts Ltd, Oxford
Produced for How To Books by Deer Park Productions, Tavistock, Devon
Typeset by PDQ Typesetting, Newcastle-under-Lyme, Staffs.
Printed and bound in Great Britain by Bell & Bain Ltd, Glasgow

Contents

List of illustrations

Breaking through brick walls

The brick walls presented by genealogy problems are challenges which can often be solved. The central idea of this book is that, however intractable a genealogy problem may appear, there is always something else that can be tried. There is also the expectation that with ever more records coming available and the development of new techniques (including genetic genealogy), problems which now seem beyond any possible solution will one day be solved.

This book offers practical ideas for solving your genealogy problems. It suggests how to make better use of the familiar genealogical records and explores some of the less common records which researchers may not use often but which provide new sources of information. With this book you will be able to make some progress on some of your genealogical sticking points.

PROBLEMS AND SOLUTIONS

There are of course problems which will remain with a solution outstanding. Sooner or later every line reaches a point beyond which it simply cannot be traced because there are not records. Or you may find ancestors did a very good job in hiding their family background. Common names frequently cause problems for the researcher. Yet with all these restrictions noted, a great deal can none the less be done.

There is a very good chance of being able to take almost any British Isles line back to the early nineteenth century, and a reasonable expectation of being able to take many lines back another couple of centuries. The utmost reach of most British Isles genealogy is the late Middle Ages – unless of course you link to the royal line or the pedigree of a handful of noble families. You may travel back half a millennium or even further before sooner or later all lines come to a point where they can be taken no further – they hit the unbreakable brick wall of a lack of records. Perhaps one day genetics will break down even this barrier, but for the moment genealogy ends with the earliest records. Before you hit that ultimate brick wall there are the sort of problems that may be solved with the ideas in this book.

Presented here is a way of thinking to tackle brick walls along with a selection of ideas most likely to be of use to solve problems of this nature. The focus is on the nineteenth and eighteenth centuries, the centuries of most genealogical research, but there is consideration of both earlier and later sources. A selection of ideas and sources are presented, those which are believed to be the most likely to break down brick walls.

COMING TO DEAD ENDS IN RESEARCH

Genealogists have come to use the term *brick wall* to mean a research dead end, the situations where family tree research does not respond to the usual tools for advancing a line and all further progress is stopped. There are two primary types of brick wall. When:

■ a birth or christening cannot be found, with the result that information about parentage is not available; and

■ a woman's maiden name cannot be found, and therefore the woman's family cannot be traced.

In addition to the problems of locating marriage and birth, evidence of movements within the British Isles or migration to or from the British Isles may not be available – moving or migration may therefore be regarded as a particular type of brick wall. There are additional types of brick wall in the tracing of collateral lines, where you are seeking to find the descendants of brothers and sisters of your direct line. There are even more problems when the research turns into a search for a living person, or is in the genealogical no man's land of the mid-twentieth century – neither a living person search nor a search for an ancestor in the period well covered by accessible genealogical records.

There is a whole cluster of brick walls relating to common names. John Smith – the most common first name and most common surname – is not going to be an easy person to trace, even if all his documentation is in order. Even names which are much less commonplace can still have far too many representatives for easy tracing.

There are also brick walls around finding the documents that bring an individual to life. Too many members of family trees are known by date of birth, marriage and death and almost nothing else, and while this may be a tidy result it is hardly an exciting one. The challenge here is to establish something of the life of the person, in effect to find some interesting documentation, or photos, or perhaps to gain an understanding of their occupation and the place where they lived.

THINKING ABOUT YOUR ANCESTORS CAN MAKE YOU SMARTER!

This is the finding of research by Peter Fischer, Professor of Social Psychology at the University of Graz in Austria, who suggests that thinking about your ancestors can make you smarter. The 'ancestor effect' seems to work because thinking about your ancestors gives a stronger sense of identity and therefore of self-esteem. Thinking about the challenges that ancestors have faced apparently acts as a spur to our own achievement.

Even more than ordinary family-tree research, breaking through genealogy brick walls offers:

- the excitement of the chase;
- demanding investigative skills; and
- enhanced awareness of personal and cultural identity.

As well as its claimed personal benefits, working on a family tree is an entry point for more academic research. The more advanced genealogical research moves out of the sphere of the independent researcher on a personal quest and enters the domain of the historian of the social sciences.

THE THREE WAYS TO BREAK THROUGH BRICK WALLS

In outline there are three (and only three) ways to break through genealogy brick walls.

1. Reanalyse material you already have and find something you have missed.

2. Find alternative ways to search records you have already searched without success.

3. Find new records to search.

Practical examples of the three ways might include the following.

1. Look at the names of witnesses on marriage certificates which you have – they are very often relatives and may provide a missing surname which you can then check.

2. Use a different search engine to search the same census records or same collection of birth, marriage and death (BMD) records. Results can be surprisingly different from what is essentially the same search on the same data.

3. If you can't find what you are looking for in a census then try a directory. If you can't find a birth registration try for a christening. If you can't find a marriage find a will in which the bride's father names his son-in-law.

The key idea is that there is (almost) always some way you can try to break down a brick wall. Only rarely will you reach a point where all avenues have been explored – almost always there is something else that might be tried.

BEING A DETECTIVE

Breaking down a brick wall is often very like playing detective and seeking to unravel a past mystery. For example, very often a research problem is hit because an ancestor did something strange in the answers they gave to bureaucracy.

Many of our ancestors wished to keep a low profile. Bureaucracy was often not trusted and individuals avoided giving information, gave the least they could, or even gave wrong information. Many felt vulnerable, perhaps because they were members of a dissenting religious group, or had a criminal record, or were a migrant, or perhaps were a member of a group that felt threatened, such as Romany Gypsies. Many were seeking to hide events in their life – an illegitimate birth, a falsified age for enlistment with the army, bigamy, separation. For a hundred and one reasons our ancestors may not have given a full and accurate account of themselves to bureaucracy.

Many in every age wished to disassociate themselves from their family. This circumstance is so commonplace that it appears to be almost a staple of family life. A high-brow literary statement of this comes from William Blake: 'A man's worst enemies are those Of his own house and family' (*Jerusalem*); very many families can offer their own personal example of a family squabble or feud.

When ancestors sought to keep their trail hidden we have to accept that they may have done a very good job. The brother of one of my ancestors, Robert Jones, emigrated from England to America and wrote a letter to his sister signing his name Robert Taylor. I have no idea what prompted this change and am amazed that his real name of Robert Jones wasn't an adequate incognito – but whatever the reason an American genealogist descended from him and trying to find the English roots of Robert Taylor is going to hit a blank. Some brick walls are real challenges to break down.

The enormous development of our age is Internet databases so, even if an ancestor had covered their tracks so well that people in their age could not trace them, it is still possible for the genealogist today to track them down.

IDEA

Start with the review

It is hardly the most exciting form of research, but it is worth while starting with a second look at the records and information you have. Sometimes the key information is on a document just waiting to be noticed. Start with the review. Then if you last searched for a record a few years or even a few months ago, try searching again. Take particular note of records which have become available recently. Basically start off your brick walls research by checking the obvious.

If this doesn't reveal the missing piece in your genealogy jigsaw, try reading this book and following up on the many ideas set out! I can't guarantee that you will break through your brick wall, but I can certainly show you some tools that might work.

2

Understanding births, marriages and deaths

All parts of the British Isles have a national registration of births, marriages and deaths (BMD), though introduced at different times in different areas and with different detail in the indexing and the certification. Genealogists are familiar with the basic concept, but understanding some of the quirks of registration and of the methodology of searching can help tackle brick walls.

WORKING WITH BIRTHS

The outline is of course simple – births are indexed by year of registration (and by quarter in England and Wales), with the registration area recorded in the index.

Throughout the Victorian age, notification of a birth was required by law within 42 days, though births could be registered without a fine up to six months from the date of birth. Births are indexed by the date of registration, not the date of birth. This can frequently be up to six weeks after the birth, and often up to six months, so births may be recorded much later than expected. Where births are recorded more than six months late they are still indexed under the date of recording, so it is possible for a birth to be listed years after it took place.

Throughout the nineteenth century there are many non-registered births, particularly in the early years of registration. In the early months of state registration (in all jurisdictions) there seems to have been a lack of awareness of the need to register a birth – in England and Wales in the last six months of 1837 around one birth in ten went unregistered (compared with the number of births in the comparable months of 1838). Late registration – after six months – was problematic because there was a fine, a situation which discouraged some tardy parents from registering the birth at all.

If you cannot find a birth it may be that it wasn't registered. The solutions are to look later (in the case of late registration) or to look for a christening, or even look instead for the birth of a brother or sister.

A quirk of birth registration is that it is possible for a birth to be registered twice – and genealogists report finding this state of affairs with some frequency. The reasons seem to be both muddle and deliberate falsification.

- The mother and father both separately register the birth.

- The birth is first correctly registered in the appropriate registration district for the place of birth then re-registered at a place which the parents consider significant. This may be the home area of the parents in cases where the birth took place away from home. Or it can even be that births are recorded in both England and Scotland (for example) so that a child can be claimed to have been born in either country.

WORKING WITH MARRIAGES

The registration of a marriage was part of the marriage process and should therefore take place on the day of the marriage. Because the registration itself was seen as an integral part of the process of getting married, registration is close to 100%.

The indexing is by each name separately. Ideally the genealogist will know both parties' names, including the bride's name previous to marriage (either her maiden name or the name of a previous husband), and will be able to look up the same entry twice, checking that the district of registration, volume number and page number are identical. It is possible to buy a certificate with the information of just one, but in doing this there is the possibility of error.

One issue to bear in mind when looking at marriages is that the age at marriage can be surprisingly young. Until as recently as 1929 in Scotland it was legal for boys of 14 and girls of 12 to marry. Throughout the British Isles marriages of women aged as young as 15 and 16 are frequently encountered – men tend to be a year or two older.

Marriages are almost always registered where they took place – but not quite always. When a marriage took place through the jurisdiction of a place of worship but not actually at that place of worship then the event is registered in the district of the place of worship. For example, the Great Synagogue in the City of London registers marriages which took place under its auspices through-out the London area – with the result that a marriage in a Jewish place of worship in Lambeth will be recorded not in Lambeth District but in City District.

WORKING WITH DEATHS

Notification of deaths is required within five days. As with births, deaths are indexed by the quarter in which they were registered, not the quarter in which they occurred, though this only rarely makes any real difference. Registration of death is close to 100% – the need for a death certificate in order for a funeral to go ahead is the reason for this.

Deaths should be recorded in the registration district where the death took place, but there do seem to be occasional exceptions – and the indexes record the recording registration district.

ACCURACY OF BMD

BMD records are the cornerstone of genealogical research – yet every researcher will have come across an event which they feel just must have taken place, but somehow isn't in the indexes. The obvious question is to wonder just how accurate the indexes are.

It is important to realize that, after the initial registration, the vital events have been copied and indexed, processes which have the potential to create errors. Many of these errors are not problematic for the genealogist. For example, where a name could not be read clearly the indexer may record it under all possible forms. Some errors are trivial spelling differences which the genealogist can usually work with. Marriages are indexed under both bride and groom and, as long as one is correctly indexed, then the marriage can be identified. Today most genealogists are using computer indexes which have been compiled by retyping (not by OCR software on a scan) – a process which offers another possibility for error.

Figure 1 Somerset House, London, once the home of BMD and probate indices, a role now largely replaced by the Internet.

Mistakes appear to be very rare – but they do exist. It is possible to check the indexes of the registration district rather than the national indexes, and the chance certainly exists that differences will be found. It is straightforward to check for a vital event in the BMD indexes of two different companies – for example in England and Wales both FindMyPast and FreeBMD have BMD records, separately compiled.

IDEA

Make full use of additional information in later BMD indexes
The England and Wales BMD give additional information in their later years, which can be crucial.

▶ *Births*: From 1 July 1911 the mother's maiden name is listed in the index. This is very helpful in making correct identification (assuming you know the mother's maiden name), and the combination of the two surnames is in most cases unique to a single family. It is possible to search for children by mother's maiden name (rather than the child's surname), which is particularly useful when searching collateral lines.

▶ *Marriages*: From 1 January 1912 the spouse's surname is listed.

▶ *Deaths*: From 1 January 1866 the age at death is given – a considerable aid in locating deaths. From 1 April 1969 the more accurate date of birth is given.

IDEA

1855 – Scotland's super genealogy year

The general registration of births, marriages and deaths was introduced in Scotland in 1855. For that first year the registration included considerably more information than subsequently. If searching a Scottish line and your direct ancestor does not happen to be born, married or died in this year it is well worth finding a sibling or even a cousin who is. The key additional information is as follows.

On birth certificates:

▶ the exact time of birth;

▶ the ages of both parents;

▶ the places of birth of both parents;

▶ the date and place of the parents' marriage (also available from 1861);

▶ the number and gender of elder siblings; and

▶ whether any elder siblings had died.

On marriage certificates:

▶ date and place of birth of bride and groom; and

▶ whether either married before and the number of children.

On death certificates:

▶ place of birth; and

▶ names of parents.

At all dates Scottish certificates and Irish certificates record more information than the English and Welsh equivalents. For example, Scottish death certificates record the maiden and all previous marriage names of a woman, and index the entry under all these surnames.

IDEA

Isle of Man and Channel Islands

If your ancestry goes back to the Isle of Man or the Channel Islands you will use the specialist guides available. The following pointers are useful for getting started.

Isle of Man

▶ Civil registration for births and deaths starts in 1878; marriages in 1884. A system of voluntary registration of non-conformist marriages existed for the period 1849–84. The Manx National Heritage Library in Douglas holds indexes, while certificates can be purchased from the Civil Registry, also in Douglas.

▶ Census records are as for the UK (save that it appears that an 1801 census was not taken) and are available online as the UK records – or in Douglas.

▶ Parish registers are, in many cases, available through the International Genealogical Index.

▶ The Manx National Heritage (Eiraght Ashoonagh Vannin) website is a key source (www.gov.im/mnh). The records they hold are extensive, including wills and administrations, property records, directories and much more.

▶ If you wish to connect with your Manx heritage you may wish to brush up on your Manx language (Y Ghailck). A great site is 'Learn Manx' at www.learnmanx.com.

Channel Islands

▶ Civil registration (all events) starts in 1840 in Guernsey and in 1842 in Jersey. The two systems are completely separate.

▶ Census records are as for the UK and are available online. Libraries on each of the main islands hold returns for all the Channel Islands. Additionally, Jersey has militia census returns for 1806 and 1815 (in French).

▶ Parish registers are, in many cases, available through the International Genealogical Index.

▶ There are super resources at both the Jersey Archives and the Priaulx Library (Guernsey). Jersey Archives has an excellent online database at www.jerseyheritagetrust.org.

▶ Until 1948 the official language of the Channel Islands was French and many records are therefore in French – in Jersey, Guernsey and Sark dialects of Norman French.

3

Finding BMD births

Records of birth are the key link for taking a line back. Often finding them is simple; these ideas apply when it is not.

AGES AND DATES OF BIRTH

Usually we calculate a person's date of birth from ages that they give at later stages in their life. Many mistakes were made in the ages given for people on the census, certificates and other documents. We all know we have to take ages with a pinch of salt, and genealogists rightly search within a few years of a calculated date. Yet the realization of the possibility of error in ages has tended to leave many genealogists with a blind spot – we all forget that most people, most of the time, got their age right.

If you have an age on two or more documents these ages can be checked for consistency. Note the exact date of an event, and the exact date of the document. If you know precisely when you are looking for a birth you are far more able to deal with variants in name or unexpected location.

INVESTIGATING ILLEGITIMACY

Illegitimacy rates fluctuate considerably and vary between locations. Around the middle of the nineteenth century

CERTIFIED COPY of an ENTRY of BIRTH.

(Issued for the purposes of the Factory and Workshop Act, 1901.)

Registration District of _Greenwich_

Sub-District of _Deptford Central_ in the County of _London_

No.	When and where born.	Name (if any).	Sex.	Name and Surname of Father.	Name and Maiden Surname of Mother.	Rank or Profession of Father.	Signature, Description, and Residence of Informant.	When Registered.	Signature of Registrar.	Baptismal Name, if added after Registration of Birth.
330	Eleventh February 1895 61 Reynolds Road	Emma Eliza	Girl	Thomas Martin	Emma Martin formerly Everson	Martin Carman	E Martin Mother 61 Reynolds Road	Twenty seventh March 1895	A J Dixon Registrar	

I hereby certify that the above is a true Copy of an Entry of Birth in a Register Book in my custody.

Witness my hand this _21st_ day of _April_ 19 _10_

Samuel Davis Superintendent Registrar

[NOTE.—The word "Superintendent" to be struck out when Certificate is given by the Registrar.]

f1021 Wt. 33004-123. 250,000. 3/10. W.H.S. & S., N. Sch. 32.

illegitimacy was around 6% of births. Given that many women in their lifetime mothered a dozen or more children, the figure of 6% indicates that very many women had an illegitimate child. Intriguingly surveys from the early years of the nineteenth century show that around 40% of the first children of a marriage were christened within nine months of the marriage – and in the West Country that figure is nearly double. There appears to have been enormous cultural acceptance that a marriage took place because the bride was pregnant. Behaviour changed towards the end of the Victorian age and into the twentieth century so that, by the first decade of the twentieth century, just one bride in five was pregnant on her wedding day.

An illegitimate child may have been given the surname of either parent, or may have been given the father's surname as a middle name. Illegitimate sons very often had their father's full name plus their mother's surname, leaving little doubt as to paternity.

IDEA

Look for illegitimate and additional children

Look for the birth (or christening) of children very soon after the parents' marriage. If you have someone you believe to be the first child born around a year after the marriage, consider that there might be an earlier child. There are even cases where the parents' marriage and the christening of the first child took place on the same day.

The position of illegitimate children was sometimes camouflaged by them being registered as a child of the mother's parents. Be alert to this scenario, especially when there is an apparent last child in a family born after a gap of years from the nearest sibling. Be alert also to a first child being born before the marriage and registered with the mother's surname, though the child subsequently used the father's surname.

4

Finding BMD marriages

Marriages can be searched for by either the bride or the groom's name. In an ideal situation you will have both and will see the same district, volume and page number recorded against each entry. The reality of course is that genealogy problems arise precisely because the full information is not available.

DEALING WITH UNKNOWN NAMES

Almost all searches are now made using online indexes. In cases where you don't know the name of one of the parties the indexes are less than ideal as only some marriages are cross-referenced to the name of the other. If you are tracing a direct line back the easiest solution is to find a child's birth certificate (which will record the name of both parents including the mother's maiden name). However, if you are tracing a collateral line, the marriage of a brother or sister of a direct ancestor, you do not have access to this information. FreeBMD offers a workaround (for England and Wales) whereby you can call up all names which are recorded in a particular volume and on a particular page. Typically this is four entries, two brides and two grooms, but if you are unlucky it may be six or eight entries. It is often possible to trace individuals in subsequent census returns and find out who married whom, and therefore resolve the issue.

Later marriages in England and Wales (after 1912) do provide the partner's surname as a cross-reference. However, the commercial online indexes presently put this information behind a pay wall. While single entry costs are low they can add up quickly if you are searching for dozens or hundreds of marriages. There may be a facility where you can input a name and the index will confirm this as a match or reject it, a useful facility if you have an idea of the name.

ERRORS ON BMD MARRIAGES

Around a half of marriage certificates contain an error. The most common are that the ages of bride or groom are wrong. Perhaps those under 21 claimed to be of full age to avoid the need for parental permission, or cultural propriety suggested that the groom should be a year or two older than the bride. Names and occupations of fathers may be wrong also – for example, many appear to give the name of the head of household in whose care they grew up rather than their real father, perhaps the name of a step-father, grandfather or uncle.

Copying mistakes in indexing are commonplace, though the circumstance where you search under two names does provide a way of finding marriages even when one name is garbled.

Marriage records remain unchanged if there is a subsequent divorce, and also if the marriage is subsequently annulled (for example, as a result of bigamy).

RESEARCHING DIVORCE AND SEPARATION

In secular terms divorce was all but impossible until 1858 – it required an Act of Parliament for each divorce. Substantial restrictions remained in place until 1945. But the religious position has not traditionally been so inflexible.

While the Roman Catholic church has been consistent in its opposition to divorce, protestant churches (including the Anglican church) have had doctrinal flexibility. The seventeenth-century writer and polemicist John Milton (perhaps reflecting his own unhappy marriage) wrote a pamphlet in favour of divorce. By the eighteenth and nineteenth centuries processes of separation existed, both informal and formal. Informally the couple simply agreed to go their separate ways (or one or the other left – for example, the wife, often to her father's home). Formally the separation may be a civil suit in the church courts. Both processes may leave a paper trail, the former simply through husband and wife residing at different addresses, the latter as a court record.

The problem of course came if either the husband or wife wished to remarry. Legally this was not possible – it was bigamy. However the religious and cultural position was less absolute. The protestant churches did not have an absolute doctrinal opposition to remarriage in theory – though they were of course aware that it was illegal – while cultural mores were perhaps more accommodating than we sometimes imagine. Couples unable to marry did live together as if husband and wife in communities where church and neighbours must have been aware of this, and often the woman took the man's surname. Children's christenings may well be recorded with nothing to indicate that they are legally illegitimate. When a genealogist has searched long and hard for a marriage and has been unable to find it the possibility has to be considered that the marriage really does not exist.

5

Finding BMD deaths

Death certificates are often overlooked. Frequently the information they give is predictable, and the excessive cost throughout the British Isles of obtaining certificates certainly discourages purchase. Notwithstanding, they can on occasions provide key information to solve problems. Important information may be found in the following areas.

- *Age at death*: more credence can generally be placed on the age on a death certificate than on a census return as the formality of registering a death encouraged people to get it right. That said the information is only as good as the informant's knowledge. Prior to 1866 (in England and Wales) it is necessary to buy the certificate to find the age – it is not in the index.

- *Occupation*: this tends to reflect the highest occupational achievement of the individual, not their most recent occupation. In the case of women the occupation is frequently given as wife or widow of a husband, with his occupation.

- *Name of the person who registered the death*: often this is a relative and may act as a starting point for investigation of a different branch. It may also confirm suspected relationships.

- *Cause of death*: while this can be vague ('general decay' or even 'old age') it is frequently precise and may give information about the number of years the person had suffered from a medical condition (for example 'paralysis, three years'). If the person is a close relative their medical history may warn you of possible health issues for you and your immediate family.

DEALING WITH AGE INFLATION

While jokes abound about people understating their age, by far the most common direction of change seems to be age inflation. People took a pride in their longevity. In particular take care with phrasing of the type 'in the 89th year of her age' which does not mean that someone was aged 89; rather, that they were aged 88. The concept is that from birth to age 1 is the first year, age 1 to 2 the second year, and so on. There are far more people who die in their hundredth year than actually reach a hundred, yet these may well be remembered as if centenarians.

INFANT MORTALITY

Infant mortality in the early years of Queen Victoria's reign was in excess of one in four. In addition to the mortality of infants (those under 5) there were high levels of child mortality. Infant mortality was usually higher in the cities than the country, and higher among the poor. It is not hard to find poor, urban communities where infant mortality was in excess of half of births. Even as late as 1921, infant mortality in the UK was still a shocking one baby in eight.

For the genealogist there is a near certainty that every generation of every family researched will have infants and children who die.

This circumstance generates documents – birth, christening, death, burial – and all these can provide useful information on the family line.

6

Census solutions

Keys to problem-solving within the census returns include the following.

■ Use the full range of the accessible censuses. Genealogists tend to focus on those of 1841–1911, and within these there is a particular focus on 1881 (because it has free access) and 1911 (both because it is the most recent and because the information is the most extensive).

■ Use 1801–31 when they are available.

■ Use other census-like surveys.

■ There are better searching possibilities within the digitized censuses.

FROM DOMESDAY BOOK TO THE CENSUS ACT 1800

The Domesday Book is of course a census. Save for this early venture into population counting, the nations of the British Isles were largely resistant to the idea of a census. The objection has long been religious. While the Bible's book of *Numbers* is indeed a census approved by God, the Old Testament describes the later census taken by King David as sinful as it sought to count the number of men who could bear arms, while Herod's census is the root cause of Jesus's birth in a stable and further cause for unease about census taking.

The first British Isles census from the years studied by genealogists is for Scotland in 1755. A project overseen by Alexander Webster required the Presbyterian ministers of every parish to count the numbers in their parish and state whether they were protestant or Catholic. The results are available today in published form as J. G. Kyd's *Scottish Population Statistics Including Webster's Analysis of Population 1755* (Scottish Academic Press, 1975). Most of what has survived is purely statistical, though in some parishes ministers collected information which included names, and which on occasions has survived.

THE CENSUS ACT

The census with which we are most familiar today is a product of the Census Act 1800: 'An Act for taking an Account of the Population of Great Britain and the increase or diminution thereof'. The first census of modern times was taken in 1801 and (save for the 1941 census, cancelled because of the Second World War) has been taken every ten years since through to 2011, which it seems will probably be the last census ever, at least in this format.

TAKING INTO ACCOUNT CENSUS DATES

The exact dates of censuses are important for calculating dates of birth from the ages given. These dates are given in Table 1.

In 1841 exact ages are given only for children up to the age of 15.

Table 1. Census dates

Census	Date
1801	10 March
1811	27 May
1821	28 May
1831	30 May
1841	6 June
1851	30 March
1861	7 April
1871	2 April
1881	3 April
1891	5 April
1901	31 March
1911	2 April

After the age of 15 ages are rounded down to the nearest five years. Someone entering their age as 40 – and therefore being between 40 and 44 years old – may have been born at any time from 7 June 1796 to 6 June 1801. Children are usually entered by their order of birth with the firstborn listed first, so the order of birth of older children can usually be determined, even when two or more children are entered as '15'. In 1841 the place of birth is given only by a yes or no in answer to the question 'whether born in same county'. This rarely causes problems of interpretation though there are a few instances of county boundary changes which may cause confusion.

From 1851 the census records the age of all, as well as a place of birth, which should be expressed in the form of parish and county. This is the basic format for subsequent censuses also. The 1911 census showed several innovations. It was the first to be completed by a member of the household (rather than by a census enumerator) and will therefore include a specimen of a person's handwriting. There were some additional questions – for example, it asked women about the duration of their present marriage. If the question is accurately answered it dates the marriage to within twelve months. It also asks how many children were born to that marriage and how many are still living.

WORKING WITH THE CENSUSES OF 1801, 1811, 1821 AND 1831

The genealogist is familiar with the censuses from 1841 to 1911 but may forget that 1801, 1811, 1821 and 1831 were also census years. Much less information was collected than for subsequent years, and most of the original returns were destroyed, leaving just statistical summaries. None the less, some schedules have survived, and there is an extensive listing of these (and where they may be found) available online at www.histpop.org/pre41/listings_a.pdf.

The 1801 census had enormous scope. As well as collecting information about the population as it was in 1801 it also required the enumerators to draw up information about the numbers of baptisms and burials every five years from 1700 to 1780, and every year from 1780 to 1800. This single census therefore reflected population not in a single year but over 101 years.

Two copies existed. The enumerators – for the 1801 census the overseers of the poor – drew up their own listings which frequently included full nominal listings for each household (i.e. a list of all names, along with their collations from the parish registers for the previous century). They then sent the required information – basically the names of heads of households and statistics for age and employment – to the London census office. These were later destroyed. However the original listings which the enumerators drew up should have been preserved in the parish chest. Some have certainly survived, frequently found today in county record offices. Many no doubt have perished. Possibly many are out there somewhere awaiting deposition in a record office. The 1801 census – and the 1811, 1821 and 1831 – may come in the future to be more frequently used by genealogists.

INFORMATION RECORDED

The information contained in all these early censuses is as follows:

- whether the house is occupied;

- name of the head of house;

- number of families in the house;

- number of males;

- number of females;

- number employed in agriculture;

- number employed in trade;

- number not employed in agriculture or trade.

Additionally 1811 required a reason for an unoccupied house, 1821 asked for some age information and 1831 had more information on occupation.

The statistics from all these censuses are available. Those most accessible are for 1831 and are available online from Staffordshire University at www.staffs.ac.uk/schools/humanities_and_soc_sciences/census/cen1831.htm.

ALLOWING FOR THE INACCURACY OF THE CENSUS

Incorrect surnames are frequently encountered. These are usually mistakes made by the census official or by subsequent transcribers. For example my own surname (Davis) appears on the 1881 census also as the misspelt versions Davies, Davy, Avis, Jarvis and Heavis, as well as the wholly inexplicable Perry, Vizzard and Martin.

Ages are notoriously misleading. Very often informants may have made mistakes. Add to this transcription error (frequently the digits 5 and 6 are confused, so someone listed as 52 might be 62). There is a common mistake around the ages of babies less than one year, often recorded as so many months old, but this figure is frequently misread to become a year, so a 7-month-old baby becomes a 7-year-old child.

In recent years census coverage has been far from 100%. For 2001 the proportion of the population captured by the census is around 94%; 2011 on some estimates has fallen below 90% – or to an estimated 79% in the London Borough of Lambeth. However, the coverage of the censuses available to genealogists is much higher, probably little short of 100%. The expectation is that your ancestors should be on the census returns. When they are not – or appear not to be – consider the following:

- A very few parts of the census returns have been lost. For example, several Fife parishes lost their 1841 returns when in 1910 the records were moved from London to Edinburgh – curiously they were moved by ship and lost at sea. Parts of the 1851 Manchester census were damaged by a flood and subsequent mould. However, such cases are very rare indeed.

- Genealogists today start their searches with transcriptions, which are inevitably subject to errors. The handwriting on many of the original returns is very poor. Those up to 1901 were written door to door, often without the benefit of a table to rest on; those for 1911 were written by the household, members of which may have had limited literacy.

- All the census returns show more babies aged between 1 and 2 years than between birth and 1. The explanation for this unlikely statistic is that many families did not feel it appropriate to enter a name for a baby until the baby had been christened. Many newly born babies are therefore missing from the census.

- Census enumerators wrote down what they thought they heard. Places of birth which are outside the local area are frequently misspelt or otherwise garbled. Unusual first names may be wrongly recorded.

- First names were considered private. There are cases where census enumerators have clearly failed to obtain this information and have written just the surname, or surname plus initial.

- Nick-names cause confusion. An online search of the 1881 census for the first name Thomas will not pick up Tom.

Similarly abbreviations can be problematic – William is frequently found as Wm, but will not be picked up in a search for William; similarly John as Jn, Robert as Rbt.

■ Wales, Scotland and Ireland frequently translate names from Welsh, Scots Gaelic and Irish to English – so in Scotland the name Alistair may appear 'translated' as Alexander.

■ The forms Mc-, Mac- and M'- are used virtually interchangeably but indexed as three separate forms.

■ Names which we may regard as separate were once regarded as if one name. This is particularly common with women's names. Thus often treated as if the same are Ann/Anne/Annie, Mary/Maria, Mary Ann/Marian, Jane/Janet (this one particularly in Scotland), Emma/Emily.

IDEA

Better database searching
Excellent database searching is needed to get the most from a particular database.

▶ Try wildcard searching. Usually * stands for any one or more letters and ? for a single letter.

▶ Soundex searching can be the easiest way to resolve spelling and transcription problems.

▶ Swap the first name and the surname in case the original form was completed with the name back to front, or a mistake was made in transcription. John Smith might be found under surname John and first name Smith. This is particularly important with surnames that resemble first names – John James can easily be recorded as James John.

▶ Search by first name alone – this can work very well when there is an unusual first name, or two first names which taken together are unusual.

▶ Search for other members of the household.

▶ Search by place of birth – this works well when the place of birth is a village.

▶ Search by address, particularly useful when you can identify an address from a certificate, directory or similar.

7

Understanding parish registers

There are of course occasions when a christening leads easily back to a marriage, and the marriage back to the christening of both parties, and so on to the next generation. British Isles parish registers are a remarkable record of the lives of the whole population over nearly five centuries. However, notwithstanding the existence of this marvellous archive and the prolific online indexing now available, the area can produce very many genealogical brick walls.

LOCATING PARISH REGISTERS

Most parish registers are now in the appropriate county record office (CRO) and are therefore among the easiest of documents to locate. A few are located elsewhere, but a straightforward Internet search for the parish name and 'parish registers' will locate these. A handful of parish registers have been published and may therefore be obtained through libraries as easily as any other book. Many more are available as photographic copies with or without transcriptions, sometimes for free, sometimes for a charge.

Parish registers currently in use are still with churches. A few of these contain old records, including some baptisms and burials dating back as far as 1813 (when new-style parish registers were introduced). Church wardens are responsible for parish registers and should be approached for access.

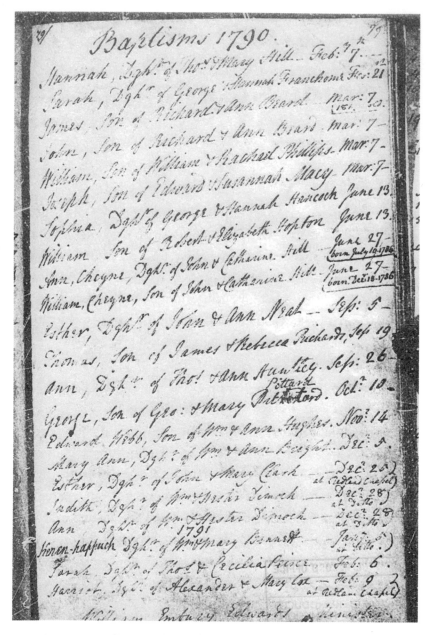

Figure 3 Genealogists familiar with searching databases which index parish registers may forget the practical difficulties of reading an eighteenth-century parish register.

DEALING WITH NAME VARIATIONS

A particular problem of parish registers is name variations, particularly in those from the eighteenth century and earlier. Name variations can be challenging. There are several types.

- Alternative names are used. Throughout the eighteenth, nineteenth and into the twentieth centuries there was a separation between the idea of the formal name given to a child and the name by which the child was ordinarily known, the latter sometimes called the 'call name'. Very often a middle name was employed as the 'call name', and often subsequently used as a first name with the previous first name either dropped entirely or becoming a middle name. Additionally there was much inventiveness in the use of nicknames. Thus Sarah can be a nickname for Cecilia, and Delia a nickname for Bridget.

- Use of Latin forms of the name. This is very common in the Roman Catholic church and is occasionally found in other sources. Often there is a direct equivalent between an English and a Latin name; a few English names have no obvious Latin form (leading to clerical inventiveness); and there are a few oddities – for example, Jacobus is the Latin for both James and Jacob.

- Use of names in the Irish, Welsh or Scots Gaelic languages.

DATES

The quarter days were, for centuries, key dates in the structure of life. Often these were when rents were due or when apprenticeships started or ended. They were busy days in the year both for commerce and for religious ceremony. Frequently christenings and marriages were carried out on these days:

■ 25 March: Lady Day;

■ 24 June: St John's Day (midsummer);

■ 29 September: Michaelmas;

■ 25 December: Christmas Day.

These dates were traditional. They do reflect the date of the solstices and equinoxes, but imperfectly. Thus the summer solstice (usually) falls on 21 June, not the 24th, so the quarter day is not in fact the longest day of the year. Similarly the winter solstice is (usually) 21 December, not the 25th. Conventionally each quarter was regarded as a season.

Our present system of starting a year on 1 January dates only from 1752. Prior to this reform the year was held to start on 25 March, the first day of spring. However, alongside this official position was a growing convention of regarding 1 January as the start of the year , and even half a century before the 1752 change people were distinguishing between the 'new year' of 1 January and the 'civil year' or 'legal year' of 25 March. Changing the year on 1 January was seen as 'new style' in contrast to the 'old style' 25 March. We still have a remnant of the civil year in our tax year, though modified from 25 March to a year end of 5 April.

The calendar is of course confusing and there is little doubt that our ancestors were frequently confused in their use of this complex system. Be aware of the possibility for confusion around the changing start date of the year, a confusion which existed decades before and after the actual change.

DIFFERENT TYPES OF RECORDS

Anglican parish registers

The church founded by King Henry VIII has shaped the character of England and played a significant role in Wales, Scotland and Ireland. It contains within it a variety of practices ranging from the High Anglo-Catholic tradition, in many ways resembling the Roman Catholic Church, through to the Low Church which more closely resembles the idea of a protestant church. In the British Isles it is the Anglican church that has been the primary record keeper, and for much of the period researched by genealogists those of all faiths, not just Anglicans, recorded their life events through the Anglican church. In the pre-Victorian era parish registers are found not only Anglicans but also most other protestants and many Roman Catholics. Just because someone is recorded in a parish register doesn't necessarily mean they are Anglican.

Methodists

This group emerged in the late eighteenth century in the Church of England. On separation they continued the recording practices of the Anglican Church, so Methodist records are in general excellent.

Roman Catholic registers

The Roman Catholic Church was at various times suppressed in the British Isles, and conventional parish registers were simply not kept. The Roman Catholic Church has at all times tended to lack systems comparable with the Anglican Church for both recording and copying parish christenings, marriages and burials.

An additional class of records in the Roman Catholic Church is those for confirmation – and confirmation records are frequently well preserved. As well as the individual's birth name they usually include also a religious name adopted by each young adult. These religious names rarely have family significance and so are of limited genealogical importance.

Protestant dissenters' records

Many protestants have found the Anglican Church to be too close to Roman Catholic beliefs and have dissented from it – the protestant dissenters. Others have sought to reform ('purify') the Anglican Church from within – the Puritans and their successors. Strictly the Puritans are from a specific period – 1559 to 1642 – but their ideas lived on in the Anglican Church for centuries, and in a form continue today.

In England the number of protestant dissenters prior to 1800 was very small – no more than 5% of the English population. In Wales, Scotland and parts of Ireland (particularly Ulster) the Presbyterian Church had a special place, and in parts Presbyterians were the majority. A feature of all protestant dissenters is the central position they give to Bible study, and a consequence is the high value placed on the teaching of literacy, including teaching women to read and write. Educated women and religious dissent are frequently linked.

In the first half of the nineteenth century the number of protestant dissenters expanded rapidly so that, by the religious census of 1851, their numbers were actually greater than the Anglican community.

Civil War dissenters and their successors

In the British Isles the dissenters grew rapidly as a result of the Civil War. The major groups are as follows.

Presbyterian

This church does not accept the office of bishop, instead vesting the government of individual churches in elders (presbyters). As a consequence of not having bishops, the majority of Presbyterian records were kept at parish level without the equivalent of the Anglican bishops' transcripts. Inevitably the survival of the single copy of most Presbyterian records has been less good than the two copies of most Anglican records. When they do survive they are frequently very useful documents. For example, christenings usually include the mother's maiden name and may include details of the parents' marriage. In cases of illegitimacy the Presbyterian Church made strenuous efforts to identify the father and to record his name.

Congregationalists

For this group the fundamental unit of church organization is the congregation, which employed ministers, often on a casual basis. The arrangement did not encourage good record keeping.

Baptists

A fundamental concept for the Baptist church is that infant baptism is invalid. Therefore a key life event recorded by other churches – infant baptism shortly after birth – is not found in Baptist registers. Adult baptisms are recorded, but almost always without information about the parents.

Quakers

Record keeping has been excellent, with the records taken extensive and many of them preserved. Marriage records were witnessed by the whole meeting, so individual Quakers are likely to be recorded on very many such certificates providing a rich genealogical tool. In the absence of a priesthood or conventional church structures, Quakers make extensive use of committees whose deliberations are minuted, along with the names of those who contributed.

Unitarians

This group refused to accept the Trinity (instead seeing God as Father alone and not as Son and Holy Spirit) and were therefore illegal until 1813. There are some records prior to 1813 relating to Unitarian societies (rather than churches).

Other groups

Moravians, Sandemanians, Swedenborgians, Inghamites, Universalists, Plymouth Brethren, British Israelites and the Salvation Army are among the many protestant dissenting groups that for a time at least attracted significant numbers. Their records are as various as the groups themselves, though in general less good than the Anglican Church. Among groups not generally accepted by the Christian churches as Christian are Mormons, found in Britain from 1837, and Jehovah's Witnesses. Individuals who were members of these groups may have their births, marriages and deaths recorded by these groups – as well as within the state system, and frequently also in the Anglican system. Additionally there may be accounts relating to an individual's spiritual journey.

Lascars

The name Lascar relates to a cultural group – sailors from India and some other destinations (particularly Yemen) who left their ships in the UK and became a working-class group within the port cities. They are found in ports (including London, Bristol and Liverpool) from as early as the seventeenth century, though they become more numerous in the nineteenth century. Ethnically they are not a single group; the linking factor is their Islamic faith. Records are exceptionally scant as their places of worship were not organized. As a male-only migration to England they inevitably married the English population, with their families subsumed within English Christianity. Burial records may specifically record them as Lascars.

Parsees

This Persian group are members of the Zoroastrian faith. They have generated some distinct records, both through their London society, the Communal House of the Religious Society of Zoroastrians (founded 1861), and through their own burial ground at Woking.

WHY PEOPLE CONVERTED

The most common reason for conversion is for marriage.

Conversion from the Roman Catholic Church to the Anglican Church is usually recorded in a parish's baptismal register, though the process was not one of baptism as the Anglican Church has traditionally accepted as valid a baptism within the Roman Catholic Church. Rather, an Anglican entry may set out that the convert 'abjures the errors of the Roman Church' (note the phrasing omits 'Catholic', reflecting the protestant view that the 'Roman Church' is not a doctrinally catholic church). Conversion from the Anglican Church to the Roman Catholic Church similarly generates a record in the baptismal register, often described as a 'conditional baptism'.

Baptists routinely accept converts through adult baptism, the same ceremony as that performed with the young adult children of Baptists. Most protestant groups have a form of baptism for converts from other churches, a process which does generate records.

Quakers have no formal conversion process. An individual may be accepted as a member of the Religious Society of Friends – or may attend Quaker meetings for many years without this membership. In the eighteenth and early nineteenth centuries Quakers required both bride and groom to be members in order to marry within a Quaker meeting – a situation that did much to reduce Quaker numbers.

First names

The nineteenth century (and before) displayed a remarkable coyness around first names. Most adults were known by their surname. Even within the family an aunt or uncle was usually addressed as aunt or uncle plus surname. Outside the family first names were rarely used. Parish registers under-record the names of women (writing instead: wife, widow or daughter of a man) and, in earlier christening records, may give only the father's name.

The terms Mr and Mrs were used as markers of respect, and frequently find their way into parish registers. In the seventeenth and eighteenth centuries Mr was often equated with a gentleman, and Mrs with the wife or daughter of a gentleman. It was therefore possible for a spinster to be described at marriage as Mrs, reflecting her father's status and not a previous marriage.

INTERPRETING RELATIONSHIPS

Descriptions of relationships are broadly those we use today. However 'cousin' once had a much wider usage, and might be applied to anyone other than a parent, sibling or child. Cousin was particularly common for relatives by marriage (for example, a brother in-law or sister-in-law might be termed a cousin). The term 'cousin german' was widely used for first cousin.

8

Finding parish register christenings

There is a long tradition of christening children very soon after birth. In the Roman Catholic Church the sacrament of christening has long been regarded as an essential prerequisite for a soul to go to heaven, encouraging the earliest possible time for christening. In pre-Reformation records in England in the sixteenth century, on those occasions where the birth date is recorded, the christening is usually within three days. The custom of early christening is subsequently found in the Anglican Church with only slight modification – in the seventeenth century most christenings are within a week or so of birth, very often on the first Sunday following the birth. Even as late as 1800 the majority of christenings are still within a week of birth.

Early christening discouraged movement far from the place of birth. Up to around 1800 the date and place of christening are for genealogical purposes near enough the same as the date and place of birth.

NINETEENTH-CENTURY CHRISTENING PRACTICE

Modifications to this christening practice occur as the nineteenth century progresses. While Roman Catholic christenings continue to be very soon after birth, the protestant churches increasingly saw a christening as a social occasion. Throughout Great Britain parishes show an increase in the number of christenings during the autumn, after the harvest had been gathered in, reflecting a time of year when people had time to gather for the christening and for the celebration that was increasingly associated with it. It is but a step to the idea of 'family christenings', a phenomenon mainly of the late nineteenth century where several children were christened at the same time.

ADULT BAPTISMS

Adult baptisms become reasonably common in the late nineteenth century though they are unusual earlier. There are three circumstances which explain why an adult baptism took place at this period.

- The person was not baptized as a child. Prior to the First World War almost all children were christened – the primary exceptions from this period are the Quakers, though the 'birth-right Quaker' would none the less have been enrolled within the Religious Society of Friends as a Quaker, generating a record of birth comparable to a christening.

- The person had been christened but not in a church and perhaps not by a clergyman. This might have been a home baptism of a child thought likely to die. Possibly doubts may subsequently have been expressed about the legitimacy of such a christening, leading to it being repeated.

- The person had been christened but the original record had been lost.

The vast majority of adult baptisms are therefore second baptisms.

An alternative motivation for a second baptism is conversion of the adult to another Christian denomination which doubts the validity of the first baptism. For example, Roman Catholic practice does not usually accept as valid baptism performed by protestant dissenters.

Adult baptisms do not often give the names of the parents (as do most child baptisms). However, they usually give either an age or a date of birth, and sometimes the parents' names are provided, especially when a preprinted form ordinarily intended for child christening was used and which provided a space for this information.

9

Finding parish register marriages

Genealogical problems around marriage can usually be expressed in terms of inability to find it. Once found the information given is often scant.

Early parish register marriages (pre-1754) record the name of bride and groom and often little else. Parish of residence is sometimes given. If one or both were under 21 years the name of the father may be recorded. Most marriages were after banns (after a public proclamation of intent to marry read on three Sundays prior to the marriage). However, banns were not formally written down and almost no pre-1754 banns have survived.

LORD HARDWICKE'S MARRIAGE ACT 1753

Lord Hardwicke's Marriage Act of 1753 (which came into effect 1754) set the framework for marriages in England and Wales.

The expectation of the Act is that on three Sundays preceding the wedding, notice of intent to marry would be given at the Sunday morning service in both the bride's and the groom's home parishes (with the bride or groom in attendance), and that these parishes would be in England and Wales. After this 'reading of the banns' the marriage would take place during appointed hours on a Sunday in either the bride or the groom's parish church, the service being conducted by an Anglican minister and with at least two witnesses present.

Very few exceptions were envisaged. Jews and Quakers were both permitted a 'Superintendent registrar's special certificate', which enabled a wedding to take place in their own places of worship. A notice in a register or on a marriage certificate that this form was used is indicative that the couple were either Jews or Quakers – though no distinction is made between the two.

Marrying after banns

Banns were to be recorded. However, the Act did not specify the form in which this should take place, and practice varied from parish to parish. Some obtained and used a preprinted book, some used an unprinted book, and some wrote banns at the back of the marriage register. The preservation of banns has been less frequent than of marriage registers (presumably as they were regarded as less important) but, notwithstanding, many do survive. Frequently they are not well indexed in catalogues – for example, a microfilm of a marriage register may include banns at the end but not clearly label them. In general banns provide less information than the marriage entry. However, as they were read in both the bride and the groom's parish there is a possibility of survival when all records relating to the church in which the marriage took place have been lost. Occasionally a special circumstance relating to a marriage might be recorded with the banns.

The reading of banns was charged for at each church where read. If the bride and groom were of the same parish there was only one charge. Very many couples claimed to be of the same parish in order to halve the charge for banns. This frequently leads to marriage certificates where both bride and groom give exactly the same address as their residence, something which is most unlikely to be the case, but was a cost-saving practice that was widely tolerated.

MARRYING BY LICENCE

The reading of banns might be replaced by obtaining a licence (properly a 'common licence', frequently called a 'marriage licence') from an archbishop, bishop, deacon or person appointed by these to issue licences. The process was quicker than banns – in theory as quick as two days. Marriage by licence was the usual practice for Roman Catholics and nonconformists who did not wish to attend an Anglican church for the reading of banns, though they were required in the period 1754–1837 to marry in an Anglican church. If a marriage is found to be by licence then it is most likely that this is a marriage of Roman Catholics or other nonconformists. A marriage licence was also needed in England and Wales if one or both were Scottish, Irish or from anywhere overseas.

Alternatively, a licence might have been used because of the speed with which it could be obtained. Typically this is when the bride is expecting the couple's first child and waiting the four weeks minimum needed for a marriage by banns may result in a child born out of wedlock, or because the husband was a soldier or sailor required to rejoin a regiment or ship. Occasionally a licence might be used when privacy was required, or by minors attempting to conceal their age. While the more affluent families could afford the higher cost of a licence, few availed themselves of this system.

PENNY MARRIAGES

Many city parishes in the nineteenth and early twentieth century offered 'penny marriages'. Typically these took place on two days in the year – Christmas Day and Easter Sunday – and were a form of group marriage. Each couple would say their vows independently, but the rest of the service was shared by several couples – who also shared the single marriage fee. A marriage which takes place in a city parish on either of these dates is most likely to be a 'penny marriage'. Genealogists report cases of documentation being confused in such marriages with a bride paired on paper with the wrong groom. As many of those marrying in these cheap weddings did not purchase a certificate and may not have been literate the mistake could go undetected.

Penny marriages which took place on Christmas Day (25 December) are easy to spot. Less obvious are those which took place on an Easter Sunday, a movable day between 22 March and 25 April, determined as the first Sunday after the first full moon after the vernal equinox (21 March). Several Easter date lists and dating calculators are available online, so it is straightforward to identify the date of Easter in any year and determine whether a wedding was an Easter Sunday wedding, but you do have to think to look. Either a Christmas Day or an Easter Sunday date along with a number of weddings in the church on that day strongly suggests a penny marriage.

MARRIAGE CURIOSITIES

There has long been a social convention that a marriage takes place in the bride's parish. This is not a legal requirement. However, the convention seems only rarely to have been breached.

It is possible for banns to be read, or a licence or special certificate to be obtained, and the marriage not to take place. If either bride or groom were under 21 they required parental permission, which may not have been given. Alternatively the couple may have been unable to afford the marriage, or one or the other may not have turned up on the day. In such cases it may still be that the couple lived together as husband and wife.

It is also possible for a couple to marry twice. If there are irregularities with the procedure of the first marriage then this may be a proper procedure to regularize the marriage. However, duplication of a valid wedding is illegal. Duplicate weddings tend to occur following an elopement, perhaps where parents accept the reality of their children's marriage and wish to have the public ceremony in their home parish.

IDEA

Multiple documents of a marriage
A marriage will generate multiple documents. Search for a brick-wall marriage using all the documents available. Typically there are three to five distinct records.

- ▶ The banns, often read in two parishes and creating two documents – or alternatively the licence or special certificate. These usually give just the names and home parishes of bride and groom.

▶ An entry in the parish register.

▶ The bishop's transcript of the parish register.

▶ The marriage certificate (after the start of civil registration).

In theory you have up to five chances to find a record of a marriage.

Civil marriages (in a registry office) do not require banns but instead an 'Intention to marry' which is posted at the registry office. Few of these seem to have survived. Marriages of Jews and Quakers generate records through these groups. Very many marriages had an announcement posted in a regional or national newspaper.

IDEA

Married with the father's consent
Marriage with the father's consent means that the individual was aged less than 21 at the time. In general this gives an age window of 17–21.

Age at marriage varies across time, and between bride and groom. Marriage ages are lowest (on average) in the eighteenth and early nineteenth centuries; they are significantly higher in the Tudor and Stuart periods, and from the mid-nineteenth century showed a trend towards increase which has continued today. In many periods there has been a tendency for the groom to be older than the bride, though by no means always – for example, towards the end of the nineteenth century there is little disparity in the ages of the bride and groom.

10

Finding parish register burials and memorial inscriptions

Brick walls around deaths usually take the form of an ancestor who appears to vanish and whose death cannot be found. Yet the practicality of the disposal of a body means that death is the most reliably documented lifetime event. Death records should always be findable!

INVESTIGATING BURIALS

Parish registers record burial rather than death, though the dates are rarely more than a very few days apart. These are the records least frequently transcribed and indexed, and are often over-looked by family historians. They can be slow to search as date of death is frequently hard to estimate, and burial can be in a parish other than that where the deceased was living, perhaps reflecting family links. Burial records have one great advantage over others – they capture a higher percentage of the population than either christening or marriage records.

The information given in burial records varies enormously. The usual basic information is full name and date of burial. Anything else is in the nature of a non-essential addition. Age is frequently given, particularly for children. The names of family members are sometimes found – particularly the names of the parents of children buried, or the name of a husband.

The cause of death is only rarely given in parish registers. When it is found it is usually a cause which is considered in some way unusual.

Perusal of almost any nineteenth-century burial records shows a surprising number of people buried who are recorded as 'name unknown'. These are often travellers passing through who died without identity and without anyone knowing their name, more often men than women but with no shortage of women. Every one of these 'unknown' people is someone's ancestor or relative whose ultimate fate is never going to be known. There are also a surprisingly large number of nameless bodies recovered from rivers and coastal waters of the British Isles.

SEARCHING FOR BURIALS IN CHURCH AND CHURCHYARD

Until 1885 (when cremation was first introduced) all British Isles deaths resulted in a burial as this was the only permitted method of disposing of a body. (Burial at sea is by definition a burial outside the British Isles and, additionally, is most uncommon.) Almost every one of your pre-twentieth-century ancestors will have been buried, and burial has left records.

Burials within a church are unusual. You are most likely to encounter them for leading local families and (in the Church of England) for the vicar and his immediate family. They are often accompanied by inscriptions and can be among the most exciting genealogical finds. The overwhelming majority of British Isles burials have taken place not within the church but outside in the churchyard, and most parish churches have surrounding church-yards which have been used for centuries of burial. A few count their use as a millennium or more, while St Paul's churchyard in the City of London counts a history of approaching two millennia, as it was in continual use from the Roman period until recent times. When you find yourself going up steps or a slope to enter a churchyard you are witnessing a ground level raised by the number of burials. Southern English churchyards (usually the most intensively used) frequently show around a foot of increased soil level per century of use.

In the churchyard graves were often not formally marked, or had wooden markers which perish quickly. Stone memorials have fared a little better, though destruction of these too has been rapid. A legible memorial inscription is a significant genealogical find.

It is practical to search churchyards yourself. However, even a small country churchyard can take several hours, and some inscriptions are only legible in good light. When a transcription of memorial inscriptions is available, use it. Local groups are increasingly undertaking this work and more and more tran-scriptions are being made. The best transcriptions are the early ones. Most of Kent is covered by a single individual's transcrip-tions from the 1920s – a strange hobby! – recording numerous inscriptions now lost or illegible.

BURIALS IN CEMETERIES

Burial in cemeteries – places unattached to a specific church or chapel – was for long associated with mass burial (for example, of plague victims). Thus a plague pit was the origin of London's Bunhill Fields cemetery – the name is a spelling of 'bone hill' and reflects the tendency for bones to surface from shallow graves. The use of cemeteries was forced on the cities of Britain by the problem of parish churchyards being overfull, yet the cemeteries themselves were rarely adequate. Up until the mid-nineteenth century cemeteries were mostly shockingly overcrowded with very rapid reuse of graves. Burials in 'plague pits' and early cemeteries have rarely left memorial inscriptions. Where later generations have placed a memorial to a worthy buried there it frequently seems that its location is little more than a guess.

New cemeteries were created in some numbers from the 1850s, and many of them are enormous. Graves in the post-1850s cemeteries are often family plots and some include memorial inscriptions which have survived, so if you can find the grave there is a chance of there being an inscription to read.

RESEARCHING CREMATORIA

The UK's first crematorium (in London) opened in 1885, with crematoria in Manchester, Glasgow and Liverpool following in the 1890s. Usage accelerated in the 1930s and has been commonplace from the 1950s.

Crematoria do maintain records which are publicly accessible. Most have details on their websites of what is available and the costs. For the genealogist the records add little or nothing to the information on the death certificate, a document easier and cheaper to obtain. Inscriptions in gardens of remembrance and memorial ledgers tend to be for the more recent cremations, and tend to be unindexed and hard to find.

IDEA

Finding cemeteries

Cemeteries often break the traditional local link between an ancestor's place of residence and their place of burial. Cities may have had a single cemetery, or boroughs within a city may have had cemeteries, either specific to a single borough or shared by two or more. In both cases the cemetery may be located outside the city or borough concerned. The best starting point is the website of the modern council for the area where your ancestor lived. Both those cemeteries which are in use today as well as those no longer in use should be detailed on the council's website, frequently with an indication of their usual catchment area. A useful website for finding cemeteries is *Deceased Online* (www.deceasedonline.com), which has information on 3,000 burial authorities and nearly 250 crematoria in the UK.

The genealogist needs to be alert to the multiplicity of names by which the same cemetery has often been known. This can reflect changing ownership – perhaps passage from private to local authority ownership – and moving municipal boundaries within a city. In London, Hammersmith New Cemetery and Mortlake Cemetery are two names presently in use for one and the same cemetery. Also in London, Deptford Cemetery was renamed Brockley Cemetery; Lewisham Cemetery was renamed Ladywell Cemetery, and for further confusion these two very large cemeteries are adjacent to one another and are now usually named as if one and called 'Ladywell and Brockley'.

IDEA

Finding graves in a cemetery
You are most unlikely to find an ancestor's grave in a cemetery simply by visiting and searching. Even assuming that the grave is marked with a gravestone (and most are not) and that the inscription is still legible, the task is daunting in scale. Many city cemeteries are a dozen or more acres in extent and contain many thousands of gravestones – searching would take days.

The use of the cemetery's records is essential. Almost all cemeteries do have lists of burials, though many are ordered by date of burial rather than name (so you need a death date to find it). Typically the records cross-reference all buried in one grave or plot, which can be a valuable family tree resource. Widows who remarried and were subsequently buried with their first husband are recorded by their second husband's surname, a circumstance which is evidence for a remarriage, perhaps not otherwise suspected.

The practicalities of searching cemeteries' records are typically that you do it yourself on site or employ an official at the cemetery to do it for you. The former often has the problem of restricted search hours and may incur charges; the latter almost always incurs charges and at a commercial rate.

IDEA

Taking full note of memorial inscriptions
Seek to maximize the information that can be gleaned from a memorial inscription.

▶ Verses can often be identified by a simple Google search and may hint at the beliefs of your ancestor. When a source cannot be identified this suggests that a family member has composed the verse.

▶ In graves intended for couples, gravestones were sometimes not erected when the first person died but when the second died. Be aware that the information relating to the first person was probably written some years after their death and with the greater chance of error that this represents.

▶ Memorial inscriptions beginning 'Here lies the body...' are centuries old and widely used in both the Anglican and Roman Catholic traditions. However, many protestant dissenters felt that the phrasing was inappropriate as it suggested an excessive veneration for the mortal remains. In its place the form favoured by many protestant dissenters – and many low-church Anglicans – was for inscriptions beginning 'In loving memory...' or 'Sacred to the memory...', which stressed that the grave was purely a memorial to the deceased. Inevitably there is much overlap. Perhaps the most that can be said is that an eighteenth- or nineteenth-century usage of a phrasing which explicitly mentions the 'body' or 'remains' implies a Roman Catholic or high-church tradition, while 'In loving memory' implies a protestant dissenting tradition. In the Victorian age new phrases are found, such as 'called to the service of the King', 'fell asleep in Jesus', 'promoted to higher service' – these tend to be dissenting. The many Victorian metaphors for 'died' ('passed away', 'called home', 'safely garnered') are more frequent within the dissenting tradition.

▶ Masonic graves from the eighteenth and nineteenth centuries are frequently marked by a skull and cross bones – though this memento mori motif is not exclusive to masons. Specifically Masonic symbols – especially the compass and set square – are also found. The Victorian age sometimes made explicit reference to Masonic beliefs in the 'Great Architect' as a name for God.

11

Using newspapers as an alternative source

One of the most exciting of the newly accessible sources for the genealogist is newspapers. The old-fashioned way of searching – by reading whole newspapers – is sometimes practical if you are looking for a specific event at an exact date. However this is only rarely possible. Rather it is the new development of digitized newspapers which can be searched quickly and easily that is opening up a whole new class of family tree records with real opportunities for solving genealogy problems.

DIGITIZATION

The process that is taking place is that newspapers are being digitized by putting them through optical character recognition (OCR) software. This creates a word-processed version of the paper, though searchers rarely see this. Rather, researchers input their search term and are offered results which lead directly to a scan of the original newspaper page.

So far only a tiny proportion of the newspapers of the British Isles (and further afield) are available digitized, but this is a new and fast-growing resource. This resource alone is transforming genealogy as a set of records of enormous importance and interest is becoming available.

TAKING ADVANTAGE OF THE GENEALOGICAL BONANZA

Among the vast quantities of genealogical information in newspapers the following areas are outstanding.

- Family announcements, primarily of birth, marriage and death, in more recent years of engagements also, plus sometimes announcements of baptism and confirmation, as well as 'in memoriam' announcements on the anniversary of a death.

- Public announcements, including the sale of land, farms, houses and livestock, often as part of the disposal of an estate by executors.

- Legal announcements, including announcements around bankruptcy, wills and divorce.

- Military announcements. This category includes the First World War practice of publishing the names of those who died on active service, and the practice of announcing officer promotions.

- Church, school and university announcements.

- Announcements of award of honours.

Additionally there is the mass of social and political comment about the times in which ancestors lived, events they witnessed and actions that influenced their lives.

RESEACHING NATIONAL AND PROVINCIAL NEWSPAPERS

The newspapers available are both national and provincial. In the British Isles most newspapers started as provincial, a term which means they were distributed in a region but aimed to carry primarily national news. Few are truly local in the way we now understand it. Provincial papers – the precursors of the nationals – are available from the early eighteenth century. Among the earliest are:

- *Norwich Post* (1701);

- *Post Boy* (Bristol, 1704);

- *Newcastle Gazette* (1710);

- *York Courant* (1715); and

- *Plymouth Weekly Journal* (1718).

At first the number of newspaper titles and their circulation was restricted by the imposition of the stamp duty tax on legal documents to newspapers, making them expensive. The number of provincial newspapers grew rapidly after 1836 (when stamp duty was reduced) and again after 1855 (when stamp duty was abolished), so the growth of provincial newspapers is largely a nineteenth-century phenomenon. Most of the nationals grew out of these thriving provincials as they expanded their distribution.

SEARCHING DIGITIZED NEWSPAPERS

Searching can be very quick, though practice within each

individual database is needed to frame search criteria in a way that yields useful results. Only the most unusual surnames can be searched by surname alone. Searches by full name (either first name, surname or surname, first name) are usually more productive. Additionally the following sorts of searches may be necessary.

- Surname plus location.

- Surname plus occupation.

- Surname of both bride and groom. Sometimes a bride is described not by name but as 'daughter of' and her father's name.

- Title plus name. Until well into the twentieth century newspapers habitually prefaced a name with a title. When the title is simply 'Mr' this is of little help, but other titles can be useful, such as 'Dr Smith' or 'Dr A. Smith'. The titles 'Miss' and 'Mrs' can be particularly useful when searching for women.

IDEA

Start with the British Library's Integrated Catalogue
The biggest repository of newspapers in the British Isles is the British Library. This contains in excess of 52,000 titles, many running to thousands or even tens of thousands of issues. Clearly this is an enormous resource. The overwhelming majority is not digitized and therefore un-indexed. Searching for genealogical information within a newspaper is therefore very slow. You do need an exact date for an event and still need lots of patience to comb through one or more newspaper issues for dates immediately following. But at least the catalogue indicates what is out there, what may be worth searching one day and what to look out for in digitized format.

If the newspaper you are interested in is one with a strong regional identity it is worth investigating with libraries in the area whether there have been any local indexing projects. There aren't many but, where they exist, they can represent an enormous time saving over trying to read even a few issues.

IDEA

Search the British Library's digitized collection
The British Library's GALE newspaper archive is readily available at www.newspapers.bl.uk. This has a selection of nineteenth-century UK national and international newspapers (49 in 2011) running to around two million pages. Some material is free; other material is behind a modest pay wall. Alternatively, the UK public library system and many other libraries have access for free. Similar collections are available from Australia (TROVE) and New Zealand (Papers Past).

IDEA

Search The Times
The Times, 1785–1985, is the most widely available UK national newspaper. It started as a 'provincial' in the sense that it was at first a newspaper distributed mainly in London, but quickly became the leading British Isles newspaper. Larger public libraries do have online access to it, as do university libraries.

IDEA

Search the ProQuest collection
ProQuest's *Historical Newspaper Collection* (www.proquest.co.uk) makes many newspapers available, most of them from the USA. Those most likely to be of interest to the British Isles genealogist are as follows:

▶ the *Guardian* and the *Observer*, 1791–2003 (previously the *Manchester Guardian*, stressing its provincial origins);

▶ *Irish Times*, 1859–2008;

▶ *The Scotsman*, 1817–1950 (and *Daily Scotsman*);

▶ *The Times of India*, 1838–2001.

Access is through library internet gateways (where the library pays a subscription to ProQuest). At present the availability of this service through UK public libraries is patchy – it may or may not be available in your area. Most university libraries do have it. The ProQuest system also includes *The Times*.

IDEA

Search the Burney Collection
This was assembled by Charles Burney (1757–1817) as a collection of newspapers and periodicals mostly from the late eighteenth and early nineteenth centuries, and running to 700 bound volumes or over a million pages. It is now digitized. The coverage is mainly London, but with some provincial, Scottish, Irish and overseas material. Access is available for free to UK further and higher education institutions through the Joint Information Systems Committee (JISC). So far it is not widely available elsewhere.

IDEA

Explore NewsVault
This is a subscription service which some libraries have, and which is particularly strong for nineteenth-century UK periodicals. It covers more than 600 periodicals and is fully searchable.

12

Getting more from wills and administrations

The transmission of property after death usually created a paper trail, and survival of wills and associated documents is reasonably good. Genealogists have long recognized their value as a key document for tracing family lines.

IS THERE A WILL?

For all sorts of reasons there may be no will or similar documentation, even when property was passed on. From the Middle Ages onwards, the custom was that heritable property was passed to the eldest son and, if this was the intention of the owner, then often no will was necessary. Sometimes a will existed and was enacted by a family without actually putting it through a legal process, therefore leaving no record. In all ages in those cases where assets were minimal it may have been assumed that the family would sort out the inheritance, perhaps reflecting an informal request by the departed.

Often, however, there is a will, even when the assets were small. One major category is men who served overseas with the armed forces, who were required to make a will. Similarly men who wished to provide for their widow or daughters needed a will and may have made a will to do just this. Many women left wills too.

There are differences between the legal systems of the nations of the UK. When there is a will the process is handled by a grant of probate (England, Wales and Ireland) or testament testamentar (Scotland). When there are assets (or debts) but no will the estate is handled by issue of a letter of administration (England, Wales and Ireland) or testament dative (Scotland). For the genealogist the practical differences are not great.

There is something of a lottery in the survival of wills and associated documents. A worst-case scenario is Devon, where almost all were destroyed. But overall the UK has something like ten million wills which have survived, plus administrations.

WHERE IS THE WILL?

Wills may be preserved at county level, nation level or in the Public Records Office (PRO). If your ancestor left assets in just one county of England, that will is likely to be preserved in the county, but if assets were in two or more counties the will may have been proved by archbishops' courts in Canterbury or York, and may have found its way into the PRO. Wales, Scotland, Northern Ireland and the Republic of Ireland tend to house wills in national repositories. In each collection, indexing and access vary significantly.

The indexing of wills and associated documents is usually inadequate for the needs of genealogists. Typically wills are indexed by the name of the testator and the date the will was proved; sometimes there is information about the solicitor. This is adequate if you know the name of the testator, though common names will need additional information of date of death. However what are not indexed are the names of beneficiaries or the names of witnesses – and it is the names of the beneficiaries and witnesses that the genealogist may know.

In many cases, wills must be viewed in person or a copy bought. The PRO has digital images available online, and this standard is being followed elsewhere, for example in Scotland and Northern Ireland. Thus in keeping with this drive for digital access PRONI has made available online around 90,000 wills as part of a project expressed in terms of a mission 'to digitise cultural resources and make them available to a worldwide audience' (Nelson McCausland, Keeper of the Records for Northern Ireland). Very many wills, particularly those for English counties, are not so far available digitally.

IDEA

What was your ancestor worth?

Wills frequently make bequests of specific sums of money, while probate on wills includes a valuation on an estate. Often it is difficult to envisage what these sums meant. Was your ancestor bequeathing a fortune or a token gift?

In theory it is possible to convert these values into estimated present-day values. *Measuring Worth* (www.measuringworth.com) has a 'relative value' calculator for the period from 1830. This offers five different ways to 'translate' wealth in 1830 into figures which are meaningful today (and each system gives widely different results). For the genealogist the most useful is the average earnings calculator. For example, this indicates that £1 in 1830 is 'worth' £829 in 2011.

IDEA

Are you a lost heir?
The possibility exists that you may be heir to a fortune. The UK publishes online at www.bonavacantia.gov.uk lists of estates of people who have died intestate and without a known heir. Where it is possible to find a relative that person will inherit – otherwise the state inherits. If you have reasonably close collateral branches with whom your family has lost contact it is possible to enter names into the BonaVacantia database and possibly identify an unclaimed estate to which you may have a claim. There are professional companies who make it their business to trace heirs of people listed on BonaVacantia, but in general they follow up only on the larger estates and on families with less common surnames. It is perfectly possible that an estate you are entitled to has passed beneath their radar – and you can claim it! Similarly there are funds from old estates lodged with the courts and waiting for heirs to come forward, listed at www.courtfunds.gov.uk.

IDEA

Finding sons-in-law
Prior to the Married Women's Property Act 1882, a married woman could not own property. A man wishing to leave a legacy to his married daughter needed to bequeath it to his son-in-law. This circumstance gives evidence for marriages which may not have survived elsewhere. If you are unsure of the maiden name of a woman it is possible to trace possible fathers, and if they left a will see if they leave a legacy to a son-in-law.

13

Directories as a census substitute

A few directories are available from the mid-eighteenth century (mostly for London) while, from the late eighteenth century, the whole of the British Isles is covered. These are a remarkable and underused source for the genealogist and a way of breaking down brick walls. They start before the census and are found for years when a census was not taken. Occasionally they provide information additional to the census.

THE RISE OF DIRECTORIES

The concept of a directory developed from lists of traders that were kept by town councils. A landmark publication is the *Universal British Directory* of 1790–99, published in five huge volumes. For every town and village this lists gentlemen, professionals (clergy, physicians, lawyers and similar) and traders, as well as a few labourers. In effect it lists selected (male) heads of households with a location and an occupation.

Directories become more common from the 1820s, with publication at first every few years but most soon becoming annual publications. Competing directory companies meant that a single location may have two or more roughly contemporaneous directories. From 1845 what became the best known series – *Kelly's Post Office Directories* – was published.

Directories were compiled by agents who went from house to house seeking information. They made no charge for inclusion – rather the income of directories came both from direct sales and adverts. A consequence of free inclusion is that almost all traders and most heads of household are included. However, the agents may have shown less zeal in collecting information in the poorer neighbourhoods, or may more often have encountered a refusal to divulge information from people suspicious of 'authority'.

LOCATING VICTORIAN DIRECTORIES

The main libraries in each locality hold a collection of directories for their own area. If you are able to visit the appropriate area this is likely to be an easy way to consult directories.

Some reference libraries are scanning a selection of early directories and making them available in pdf format. While a welcome step towards better access, the process is far from perfect.

- Many of the original directories have faded ink on yellowing paper which impedes scan quality.

- Many libraries use a low-quality scanner and may have it set on a fast-scan setting which results in lower quality.

- Those I have seen are made available on a library intranet, not on the Internet, so you cannot search from your home computer.

In effect by this process libraries have replaced a fragile, paper directory with an imperfect scan and have not removed the restrictions on access. It is good for preservation but not for ease of access.

The great advantage of a scan is that it can be searched using the pdf search facility – but be aware of the restrictions posed by poor scan quality. A search for a surname may fail to turn up that surname even when it is present in the directory.

A better option is often the collection of directories available through *Historical Directories* (www.historicaldirectories.org), which offers a representative cross-section of directories sorted by date and location.

IDEA

Universal British Directory (1790–99)
Few libraries have this directory (it is a rare book) and, at the time of writing, there is not an easily accessible online version – for while the London volume has been digitized it appears that it is accessible only through academic subscription services, basically through university libraries. Presumably this situation will be remedied soon.

Notwithstanding the difficulties of access it is worth seeking this directory. If you have a line traced back to the 1790s it is likely that you will find reference to them in this source – while it isn't 'universal' it is extensive in its coverage.

IDEA

London Lives
Not itself a directory but taking much information from directories is the database *London Lives, 1690–1800* (www.londonlives.org), which has around a quarter of a million records relating to Londoners in the eighteenth century. The database is searchable by an ancestor's name.

14

Electoral roll as an alternative source

Democracy has created a substantial paper trail. Poll books and the electoral roll are so far available almost entirely in printed formats which are not particularly quick to search, though digital formats are coming. These are significant sources for genealogy. Painstaking work can already use them to solve problems, while the forthcoming digitization will make them a major genealogical source.

SEARCHING POLL BOOKS

A 1696 Act of Parliament made the compilation of a list of voters compulsory, and these were usually printed. From 1696 to 1872 (when the secret ballot was introduced) poll books were created and (at least from 1711) have usually survived.

Poll books are not standardized – the information varies from area to area, and from year to year. Typically the minimum information given is the elector's name and how his vote was cast. Usually there is an address also (though this may be simply the name of a village) and there may be information on occupation and the voting qualification. In general poll books are not indexed and are not in alphabetical order of electors. They can often be searched by village or by street address if you know the precise location of your ancestors. Alternatively a region or town can be searched in its entirety simply by looking down the list. They are not quick to search.

THE TRADITIONAL UK ELECTORAL SYSTEM

For many centuries each county of England and Wales and later on the whole UK returned two Members of Parliament to Westminster – called Knights of the Shire. Additionally the towns and cities – the boroughs – had their own representatives. In both counties and boroughs the MPs were elected by those who met a qualification to vote, the suffrage.

THE WESTMINSTER ELECTION 1796.

Figure 4 Hustings: did your ancestors who lived before the Great Reform Act vote?

SUFFRAGE

In England and Ireland eligibility to vote (or voting qualification) was established in 1430 on the basis of owning property which produced an annual income of 40 shillings or more. This basic qualification remained unchanged at 40 shillings until 1832. A few parts of the UK even used the qualification until 1918, nearly five centuries after the system and the tariff had been established.

The basic requirement to vote was to be a man over 21 years of age who owned property estimated to be worth a rent of more than 40 shillings per year. However, alongside this basic requirement there were many local systems which gave the vote to additional people. Typically possession of a certain property gave a vote, even when the value of that property was under the 40 shilling threshold.

One alternative qualification for voting in some boroughs was dwelling in a home which contained a hearth big enough to wallop (boil) a cooking pot. Such voters were called potwallopers. The system continued until 1801 in Ireland, and until 1832 in England (it seems it was never a part of the Welsh or Scottish systems). Of course just about all homes did have a hearth big enough to boil a pot, at least a small one, so the potwallop was a very wide suffrage. Was one of your ancestors a potwalloper?

The complex system was simplified by the Great Reform Act 1832, which created a much simpler qualification for voting. Subsequent reforms in the hundred years or so following increased the number of people who could vote. Immediately after the Great Reform Act 1832 about one man in five was on the electoral register. By 1869 this had risen to around one man in three.

Very often – both before and after the Great Reform Act – there was a rough-and-ready equivalence between being the head of a family (in whose name property was held and rents paid) and being a voter. In any period around half of families are represented by their head appearing in a poll book. While this is very far from our universal suffrage it was a functional democratic system in which most of our British ancestors' families will at various times have taken part.

EXCLUSION OF ROMAN CATHOLICS

A restriction of the suffrage was that it was for many years not extended to Roman Catholics. These restrictions had been introduced because the popes refused to recognize the right to rule of the protestant, Hanoverian kings. The logic of exclusion was that a person whose faith did not recognize the legitimacy of the king to rule could neither be an MP nor vote for an MP. However, the restriction continued even after the papacy's decision in 1765 to recognize the legitimacy of Hanoverians. Parliament moved in 1829 to address the situation but, instead of wholly removing the exclusion, introduced a voting qualification for Roman Catholics different from that of non-Roman Catholics. The traditional requirement of owning property worth 40 shillings a year (£2) was replaced by a special requirement for Roman Catholics that they should own property worth £10 a year. This decision in effect disenfranchised most people in Ireland, where the prevalent Roman Catholic faith (along with the custom of dividing land between all heirs) meant that very few people met the voting requirement. The Irish electors were effectively only resident, protestant, 40-shilling freeholders and absentee landlords.

VOTES FOR WOMEN

Just a century ago only men could vote. Women gained the vote in 1918, in part reflecting the changing occupational roles of women through the First World War, and in part the campaigning efforts of the suffragettes. At first the suffrage granted to women was different from that of men. While a man merely had to be over 21, a woman had to be over 30 and, additionally, had to pass a property qualification. Equalization of the male and female suffrage waited until 1928.

Figure 5 The suffragettes' campaign for Votes for Women resulted in women voting from 1918.

RESEARCHING MODERN ELECTORAL ROLLS

Public libraries do hold the current electoral roll for their local area and frequently hold a selection of earlier electoral rolls. These are indexed by street, not name, so they are rarely quick to use. Additionally there are restrictions on copying a current or recent electoral roll – for example, libraries will not permit photocopies, and many are alert to prohibit even the copying out by hand of more than an entry or two. Many libraries extend these restrictions to all electoral rolls, irrespective of age.

DIGITIZATION OF ELECTORAL REGISTERS

There is an agreement for all electoral registers from 1832 to be digitized. This work is being undertaken by FindMyPast and will undoubtedly be a major asset for the genealogist – when it is completed in a few years' time.

IDEA

Finding poll books
Good sources include the following:

▶ local libraries;

▶ major regional libraries;

▶ the Society of Genealogists;

▶ the Guildhall Library;

▶ the Institute of Historical Research;

▶ the British Library; and

▶ online.

IDEA

The modern electoral roll online

The modern electoral roll is available online, for example, through *Trace Genie* (www.tracegenie.com), which offers 24 hours of access for a low, non-recurring subscription. It is also accessed by many other search services, including www.192.com. With the modern electoral roll you can track down a recent address of (almost) any adult in the UK whose name you know – or draw up a list of all possibilities if the name is common. Bear in mind that electoral roll opt-out has been possible from 2002, so the most recent rolls are not quite comprehensive.

Trace Genie also offers 24 hours of access to the England and Wales BMD, 1984–2005, for the same subscription.

IDEA

Modern reprints of poll books

A few poll books have been published as modern books. For example, the series *Raymond's Original Poll Books* (published by S.A. and M.J. Raymond) has facsimiles of poll books including London, Westminster, Norfolk, Somerset, Suffolk and Yorkshire. Publisher Spindrift has some Cambridgeshire titles. The Parish Register Transcription Society has a few poll books available (for purchase) on CD, including Brighton, Lewes, Southampton and East Kent.

15

Other alternative sources

When the major genealogical sources of BMD, census and parish registers fail – or when you want more information – you need to look at alternative sources. This is a key method for breaking down brick walls.

SEARCHING CENSUS SUBSTITUTES

The Return of Owners of Land of Over One Acre in Extent of 1872–76 covers all four countries of the UK and is available as a set of books through the largest libraries. It contains 302,023 names representing a high proportion of rural households for the period. The information provided is the landowner's name (usually including the forename though sometimes just initials), address, the extent of land measured in acres, rods and poles, and the estimated rental value.

SOCIETY OF GENEALOGISTS

Founded in 1911 to 'promote, encourage and foster the study, science and knowledge of genealogy', this London-based society has a massive library of records for the genealogist, including very many that are unusual or unique. It is available either by annual subscription or on payment of a daily search fee. The coverage is primarily the British Isles, though with many Empire and Commonwealth records also. The starting point for most is to consult their catalogue (www.sog.org.uk) to see whether there is a source which looks promising for your brick wall.

RESEARCHING CORONERS' INQUESTS

The coroner is one of the earliest public offices. A coroner's inquest is held whenever there is a sudden death, or a death which is considered in some way suspicious. It is both a medical and legal investigation with a principal aim of the increased detection of murder.

In the UK up to 1926 a coroner's inquest was held before a jury. It therefore generated a considerable paper trail and very often had press coverage. A coroner's inquest expected to establish the identity of the deceased, how, where and when they died, and additionally (if the verdict of the inquest was murder or manslaughter) to identify the person to be tried.

Coroners' inquests were very common. They were prompted, for example, by an accident leading to death (frequent in the factories of industrial Britain), by all sudden deaths, by possible suicide, by many cases of infant death where infanticide was suspected, by abortion (which in legal terms was seen in much the same way as infanticide and could in early years leave the mother facing the death penalty) and by much else.

USING LAND TAX INFORMATION

The Land Tax was an annual charge on all land payable to the government. Its heyday was 1692 to 1868 though there was some collection both before and after. The best survival of records is for the period 1780–1832, the period during which the Land Tax register and the electoral register were linked. For this period there is near complete coverage.

The information given under each parish is the name of the owner of a parcel of land, the occupier of that land, often the name of that land, and the annual rental charged. In many cases the parcel of land is small. In rural areas the Land Tax approaches the status of a census of heads of households. Many landowners and tenants appear twice or more times if they own or occupy distinct parcels of land.

The difficulties with these records are twofold.

- They are often Cinderella records which may not be clearly catalogued in collections. Identification of holdings may therefore be problematic. They are rarely digitized so in general need to be consulted at a record office.

- They are ordered by parish, not person, so identifying people you are interested in may be a lengthy search.

Once an entry has been found the biggest area of interpretation is what the rental value means in terms of acres of land. Rents depend on the locality and the time, so there is no automatic conversion formula. Local historians may have studied the Land Tax and made an assessment. Alternatively you need to identify in the return several people whose land holdings can be quantified from other records and calculate a rough equivalent.

VACCINATIONS

It is possible to access your own vaccination and immunization record (along with your health records) through a freedom-of-information request – if the records have been preserved. You can access someone else's records with their permission. Vaccination records from a century and more ago are sometimes available, though there is a lack of clarity in terms of what has and has not survived and inadequate indexing.

The records most likely to be of interest to the genealogist are vaccination for smallpox. During the eighteenth century around a third of all deaths and most child deaths were caused by smallpox. Smallpox vaccination dates from 1796. From 1841 free child vaccinations were available (though uptake was not particularly high) while, from 1853, the vaccination of children was compulsory. The process created a paper trail.

Nineteenth-century vaccination records record the following:

- the date of the vaccination, and by whom performed;
- the child's name, age and address;
- the name of the child's father.

SEARCHING OLD AGE PENSIONS

The Old Age Pensions Act 1908 introduced pensions paid by the state for all aged over 70 who were judged to need it. Previously a few men and a very few women had private pensions or pensions linked with occupations, but these were unusual – the majority of pensions were military pensions. Most people in their old age continued to work, were supported by their children or received poor relief through the parish or the workhouse.

The first old age pensions payments were made on 1 January 1909 (in England, Wales and Ireland; 2 January 1909 in Scotland reflecting the bank holiday there). They were made during a particularly bleak winter which emphasized the need for just such an old age pension. The newspapers described the first payment as 'Lloyd George's New Year's gift', reflecting the work of Chancellor Lloyd George in steering the legislation through Parliament. Payment was handled by the post office, with the expectation being that those eligible would collect their pension in person. It seems that the first ever state-pension day became something of a national festival as many claimants put on their Sunday best for their trip to the post office. It is reported in several newspapers that Mrs Rebecca Clark, aged 103, 'walked briskly' to the post office to collect her pension.

The old age pension was means-tested on a sliding scale of payments, with the most affluent receiving nothing – but the great majority were eligible. Claimants were issued with a pension book which identified them and – crucially – proved their age.

The proof of age was frequently a difficult issue. In order to claim a pension on the first pension day it was necessary to be born on or before 31 December 1838. In England and Wales the registration of births had started on 1 July 1837, so for this eighteen-month period it was in theory possible for an English or Welsh claimant to produce a birth certificate. However, there were a significant number of early births not registered – within the ball-park of one in ten – while certificates had frequently not been purchased at registration or had been subsequently lost, while women who had married also needed a marriage certificate in order to document their change of name. For Scotland and Ireland civil registration is later; for England and Wales there is no civil registration prior to 1 July 1837. Thus parish registers frequently needed to be used. The responsibility for proving age was that of the claimant, with claimants asked to provide documents. A great variety were accepted, including even family Bibles.

For the genealogist the key piece of information in early pension books is a precise date of birth, something which may be hard to find from other sources. They also give the full name and address.

IDEA

Finding pension books
There is no central repository of pension books. However, some are available, particularly from the early years. The three key places to look are:

▶ county record offices;

▶ the National Archives; and

▶ the British Postal Museum and Archive (www.postalheritage. org.uk).

GETTING MORE FROM LIBRARIES

Libraries in the British Isles fall into the following categories.

■ The public library system in the UK (and equivalent in the

Republic of Ireland). This superb resource includes the Inter-library Loan system which will deliver almost any book held in the UK to your local library. There is a small administrative fee.

■ Local studies centres, part of the public library system, offer a range of materials for their locality as well as some national coverage.

■ University libraries frequently hold specific collections which relate to the social history of their area. Access (without borrowing rights) is usually straightforward.

Private libraries are relatively unusual, but there are some remarkable exceptions. For example, the Literary and Philosophical Society (Newcastle) – known simply as the 'Lit & Phil' – was founded in 1793 and has an extensive local collection for the north-east of England. A unique resource is the society's membership records which cover a significant fraction of the people of nineteenth-century Newcastle and beyond. The library is strong in regional directories and parish register copies.

16

Yet more sources: the Freedom of Information Acts and the genealogist

The UK benefits from legislation which grants access to information held by public bodies. This is through the Freedom of Information Act 2000 for England, Wales and Northern Ireland, and the Freedom of Information (Scotland) Act 2002, both coming into force in 2005. Although the legislation has now been in place for a few years the process of people becoming aware of the powers these Acts grant has been relatively slow, while modifications to access systems used by public bodies is an ongoing process.

The system is simple – you make a request for information (usually using an online form) and the body is required by law to reply, and usually to provide the information. There is a fee (presently £30) which may be waived if the cost to the organization of providing the information is low.

ACCESSING MILITARY SERVICE RECORDS, 1921–97

The system applies only to public bodies. It has to be said that the vast majority of records which can be accessed through the provision of the Freedom of Information Act are unlikely to be of interest to genealogists. But there are some, for example military service records from 1921 to 1997 (and including the Second World War), that are usually available and may be accessed by the person concerned, their next of kin and certain other close kin. It may take two to three months – welfare inquiries are prioritized and genealogical requests are understandably the ones that tend to go to the back of the queue. The records are typically rather brief, so may not be the genealogical breakthrough you might hope for. However, the system does mean that there is now access to military service records that was not possible prior to 2005.

LIMITS TO FREEDOM OF INFORMATION

The system is beginning to expose some oddities in access to records of interest to genealogists. For example, the General Register Office (GRO) (which provides birth, marriage and death certificates in England and Wales) is a public body and it may therefore be reasonable to think that they would be required to provide information under the terms of the Freedom of Information Act. As the cost of providing information where exact details are given is very low it may appear that the information should be provided for free (in contrast to the charges made for certificates). In fact the Freedom of Information Act gives an exemption for 'information which is reasonably accessible to the applicant otherwise than under [the Act]', and access on payment of a fee (currently £10) is considered to be 'reasonably accessible'.

But consider the case of a search for the birth of a John Smith in 1885, in a circumstance where you know parents' names and could identify the right birth certificate when you see it. There are 528 such births in 1885 alone. As the GRO has withdrawn its search service the only way to access the information is by purchasing all certificates at a cost of £5,280. It seems to me that the price is such that the information cannot be regarded as 'reasonably accessible' and that there is a case for requesting it as a £30 freedom-of-information request. So far no one appears to have tried.

IDEA

Exploring the Freedom of Information Act
You can make and explore freedom-of-information requests at the official site (www.whatdotheyknow.com).

17

Publishing your family tree

Brick walls can be broken down if other researchers can access your materials and comment on them. Ultimately a family tree is a collective endeavour, and publication in one form or another is essential.

ONLINE TREES

Very many genealogists publish their research online through commercial sites. The big ones that you will certainly want to consider include:

- Ancestry (www.ancestry.co.uk);
- FindMyPast (www.findmypast.co.uk); and
- GenesReunited (www.genesreunited.co.uk).

Sites such as these offer the easiest method to publish a tree and, as a result of their size, are the places where your tree is most likely to be seen.

PUBLISHING YOUR FAMILY TREE AS A BOOK

Publication is also possible in book format. While you are most unlikely to find a commercial publisher for such a book, the introduction of print-on-demand, self-publishing services means that it is reasonable to produce your own book. If you want to try this route it is straightforward.

A caution is that there are restrictions on publishing information about living people. Publication means in the public domain and, as such, you should therefore be very careful as to what is made available about people who are alive. You may also wish to apply sensitivity on issues which have the potential to upset, which in practical terms means that you don't have to tell every story.

The publication process is one where you upload your files for the book, typically in the form of a word-processed file with embedded illustrations. You can design your own cover, select an off-the-peg cover or accept professional design. Most self-publishers issue an ISBN number. If the number is in the UK system a copy of the book will be lodged with the British Library, which in effect means preservation for ever. Costs are very low. A ball-park figure is £100 for the services of the self-publishing provider and around £10 for copies (more for hardback or colour illustrations). It is possible to set the price so as to pay you a royalty and, if you can sell a few dozen copies commercially, you may even recoup your outlay.

Books remain in print indefinitely and are usually listed by online bookshop Amazon, so it is easy to obtain additional copies if you or anyone else needs them. Online formats including Kindle are also available but don't generate an ISBN and therefore are not automatically catalogued and preserved by the British Library.

WRITING YOUR FAMILY HISTORY

Publication is the easy bit! What is hard is writing the book. Family trees don't easily fit the linear format of a book.

- The most common format is an account which follows a single family line from earliest records to most recent. In effect this leaves out most information about the spouses who marry into this main line.

- A modification of the single family line model is a one-name study which seeks to trace all collateral lines. In effect this format needs to look at each main collateral line separately. It can be repetitive.

- Tribute volumes describing the family of a single individual can be attractive. Typically a number of lines are traced backwards from most recent to earliest. A final section may look at descendants.

- Writers may try to find a wider readership by developing themes of social and local history around a family line. This works best for a family living many generations in one location or following similar occupations over generations.

- Where a family are associated with a particular building over generations the history can be both of the family and the building.

A format which may work for many writers is a series of short chapters (mostly around a single individual) each supported by an illustration.

DISTRIBUTING YOUR BOOK

Distribution may be as simple as printing half a dozen copies and giving them to family members. Other options include the following.

- Ask appropriate libraries to shelve a donated copy. Most local studies centres will accept material relating to their area.

- Select a title which includes appropriate keywords. This may well be a long title, or a title plus subtitle. Typically you want in the title the family surname, the location (perhaps expressed both as village and county or area), an indication of the time period covered, perhaps something about key occupations.

- If your book is listed on Amazon make sure you set up the keywords. If the publisher has not provided Amazon with a picture of the cover you can do this.

- Make sure that online boards with an interest in a surname know that your book exists. You may need to ask permission to post an entry on a book as it may be perceived as commercial.

For the genealogist, a published family history both preserves information and reaches people who may know more. So that you may be contacted, remember to include your email address.

18

Oral history

Genealogists like their documentary sources. Yet oral history can be every bit as valuable.

Most genealogists start their research with the memories of family members, a form of oral history. Often family information can be the key to getting back to 1911, the most recent of the available censuses. Very many people alive today have parents and grandparents on this census, and very often these people are remembered. A mass of family information, along with social and local history, is available through oral history. Sometimes family memories can be very long indeed, and family traditions can be preserved for very many generations. The longest I have personally come across is a family memory of three hundred years, or ten generations. There is a clear need for oral history to be sought and where possible recorded – and in this the genealogist can play a part.

There are also areas of family history research where oral history is the crucial source. For example, Romany Gypsy genealogy is an area where oral history may be the key to success. Romany families have a tradition of avoiding bureaucracy and therefore avoiding creating written records, along with a strong sense of family identity that has promoted an oral tradition. It may well be that written records do not exist but oral histories do, and the oral history may plug a gap.

Assessing the Accuracy of Oral History

There is, of course, no simple answer to the accuracy of oral histories. The most problematic area is that of family traditions which have been handed down through several generations. The process is akin to Chinese whispers – things get altered. The simplest alteration is the generation of an event – something reported as happening to someone's grandfather actually happened to their grandfather's grandfather. There is a tendency for a story to be remembered but not the name of the person associated with it, the dates or the exact places – all frustrations.

Finding Oral History

As far as I can see there is no centralized repository of British Isles oral histories. Until such comes into existence the resource is going to be hard to access. A problem is that the law does not encourage such a repository. Oral history is governed by two key Acts:

- the Copyright Act 1988, which restricts all editing and adaptation;

- the Data Protection Act 1998, which requires written permission for publication, usually given through a 'clearance form'.

Most oral history cannot demonstrate compliance. If you do record your own oral history or that of a relative it would be sensible to ensure that you make or obtain a written statement giving permission for publication so that at some stage the 'archive' can be made available.

IDEA

Try YouTube

Personal recollections of twentieth-century events are now to be found on YouTube (www.youtube.com). Additionally, YouTube offers a free and easy way to preserve and make available your own or your family's oral history.

19

Local history

The study of local history has been transformed from the hobby of people connected with a locality into an academic discipline. Where once local history was usually little more than an antiquarian assemblage of available facts it is now governed by sound historical theory and a careful approach to evidence, frequently using quantitative methods. In a nutshell, local history has been updated just as much as the study of family history.

Local history needs to be approached with caution and with the warning that much local history is better regarded as antiquarian. By antiquarian is meant that it is a collection of facts, figures and stories without much effort to check their veracity, to ensure a reasonable coverage of topics or to offer objective assessment. Bluntly, much published local history is bad history.

It is, therefore, particularly important to be aware of those societies which promote sound local history study. The leading local history society is the British Association for Local History (www.balh.co.uk), which publishes two journals, *The Local Historian* and *Local History News*. This association promotes the study of local history both as an academic discipline and as a leisure pursuit, and is therefore part of the process of bridging the gap between the hobbyist and the academic. The work of local historians is increasingly seen as a way of testing the assertions of professional historians by asking whether the generalizations of the professionals really are supported on the ground at local level.

LOCAL HISTORY SOCIETIES

Inevitably the study of local history has produced local history societies, and there can scarcely be a locality in the British Isles not now covered. Virtually all have a website, so finding them is usually straightforward, and the website may well contain information of interest to genealogists with lines in that locality.

EXPLORING LOCAL HISTORY TOPICS

Frequently encountered local history topics that are likely to be of interest to the genealogist include the following:

- the Poor Law and the workhouses in a locality;

- crime and courts, particularly crime with a regional interest (for example, smuggling, cattle theft, poaching);

- the home front in the First and Second World Wars;

- local photographs, including buildings, occupations and people;

- nonconformist religious groups in a locality.

RESEARCHING LOCAL HISTORY SOURCES ONLINE

Frequently local history groups create databases, and frequently these are of some value to family historians also. There is a wealth of material available, yet the genealogist needs to approach it with caution for while there is excellent material much is indifferent or simply wrong. A checklist for assessing the reliability of a local history website includes the following.

- Does it appear to be carefully constructed? Sites with typographic and presentational errors are most likely to contain factual errors also.

- Is there a clear author, either an individual or a society? Named authorship suggests a degree of professionalism.

- Why was the site constructed? Many are commercial, promoting businesses in an area, and many of these favour sensational stories rather than sound history.

- When was the site last updated?

- Are the sources made clear?

USING TITLE DEEDS

Title deeds are a bedrock source of local history and an enormous resource usually ignored by the genealogist. They contain enormous quantities of genealogical information including the names of owners, tenants, trustees and witnesses – a substantial proportion of a community. They are frequently linked with family settlements and marriage settlements. The family settlement allowed a landowner to divide his land between his children while still alive – in effect they are like a will – while a marriage settlement is usually a dowry given at the time of a daughter's marriage. Such documents contain information about two or more generations. For example, marriage settlements typically contain the name and residence of both husband and wife along with the husband's occupation and frequently the name and occupation of both fathers. When the dowry being given is that of the bride's mother the marriage settlement of the parents may be appended.

In a nutshell, title deeds and associated records can be a superb genealogical source. However, they are also a difficult source.

- Finding collections is frequently difficult. There are collections in CROs, the PRO, reference libraries nationwide, some universities (for example, the University of Nottingham has an extensive Nottinghamshire collection), the British Library, the national libraries of Wales, Scotland and Ireland, the Bodleian Library (Oxford), Cambridge University Library and doubtless many other locations. Many title deeds are in private hands, linked with the land to which they relate, as well as bought and sold by collectors.

- Finding relevant documents within a collection can be difficult. Often indexing is imperfect, with many documents indexed only by a lead name.

- Reading title deeds can be difficult. Many – even some that are not so very old – are in Latin. Handwriting issues can be particularly difficult.

- Understanding the documents can be difficult as they are legal texts. Those for England and Wales are in one legal system; Ireland is in essentially the same system; Scotland is in a completely different Roman Law system.

- The family tree information from a single title deed can often be scant. They are usually useful cumulatively – which of course presents problems of locating more deeds.

LAND TENURE AND TITLE DEEDS

The system in England, Wales and Ireland is that land was held in a variety of tenure types. Some of the most common are as follows.

■ Freehold – the term is with us today.

■ Copyhold – land held by possession of a copy of a court roll is a type of manorial landholding where a person owned the property but paid some charges to the manor. Most were converted to freehold in the nineteenth century (they were 'enfranchised'); those that survived were abolished in 1922.

■ Three-life lease – a lease with a duration of three lives, or up to 99 years. This type of title deed may well contain much genealogical information.

■ Quitclaim – the custom of property being passed by inheritance was so strong that ownership of property sold could be contested by a relative who might have expected to inherit it. The sale of property was therefore often accompanied by a document from the potential inheritors agreeing to quit any claim.

IDEA

Considering local history
When you consider local history, read:

▶ what is now the standard book on bridging the gap between local history and genealogy: *From Family History to Community History*, edited by W.T.R. Pryce (Cambridge University Press/Open University, 1994);

▶ a seminal book on English local history: *Ambridge: An English Village through the Ages*, by Jennifer Aldridge and John Tregorran (Eyre Methuen, 1981).

IDEA

Finding local histories

Available through the UK public library system is *The Victoria History of the Counties of England*, dedicated to Queen Victoria and published from 1899. Most counties are covered by several large volumes. The biggest advantage of this series is its accessibility – wherever you live in the UK (and beyond) the whole set is usually available, with even many libraries of modest size holding a set. The scope is enormous – including prehistory, topography, Domesday Book, people and buildings – and it is undoubtedly worth a look.

An early published local history source is William Camden's *Britannia*, which has coverage of the whole of the British Isles. Its intention was 'to restore antiquity to Britaine, and Britaine to its antiquity' and as such it offers an extensive assemblage of regional antiquarian information.The first edition (1586) was in Latin, though subsequently translated into English by Philemon Holland (1610). Later versions are in English. These are:

▶ 1695 by Edmund Gibson; and

▶ 1789 by Richard Gough (revised 1806).

The 1610 translation is readily available on the *Vision of Britain* website (www.visionofbritain.org.uk).

IDEA

Reading local histories

What is available varies enormously, but can be richly rewarding. For example, *Glimpses of Our Ancestors in Sussex with Sketches of Sussex Characters, Remarkable Incidents, &c* by Charles Fleet was published in 1882 by a local publisher (Farncombe & Co, Lewes). In its entirety the book is hardly bestseller material (though it did manage a second edition); as an antiquarian assemblage of other people's observations it is fascinating. There is some factual information about occupations – for example, in this description of a Sussex shepherd's first work:

> When I was eight years old I began to follow the sheep during the summer months; in winter I sometimes drove the plough.
>
> (reminiscence of John Dudley of Rottingdean, born 1782)

Much of the book is description of a rural lifestyle just a step above poverty:

> A body more spare than that of our Sussex cottage-wife is rarely to be met with that is in a sound, healthy body, which, as was her boast, had never known a day's illness since it could take care of itself … Lines of beauty, physically, there were none; but morally, in the absence of all thought of self, Mrs Colly was a line of beauty from the top of her head to the soles of her feet … A type of a class that was once common in Sussex.
>
> (1870s description of Mrs Colly, then in her 70s)

> In their persons not corpulent, but rather spare and thin-shanked; in their diet generally frugal; and in their cookery, being neither dainty nor expensive, they care most for pork, which, indeed, they prepare skilfully by steeping in brine.
>
> (description of the people of Sussex by Dr Burton of Cambridge, 1751)

IDEA

Sunday school registers

Sunday school registers and other records have not survived in great numbers and they are not easy to locate. They are a feature of the nineteenth century, and of the cities more than the rural areas. Teaching included both Christianity and reading and writing. The basic genealogical record that they offer is an attendance list. Children were usually from families linked with the church associated with the Sunday school – but not necessarily so. Many parents valued the free education given by a Sunday school and were not too concerned about its denomination.

20

Descriptions of an ancestor's home

One of the most evocative sources for an ancestor's life can be a contemporary account of that location. An eighteenth-century example is the extensive writing of Arthur Young:

- *A Six Months' Tour through the North of England* (1770);

- *Farmer's Tour through the East of England* (1771);

- *A Six Weeks' Tour through the Southern Counties of England and Wales* (1772); and

- *Tour in Ireland* (1776–79).

Arthur Young was a Suffolk-born writer and economist best known for these descriptions of tours he made through England and Ireland, which focus on agricultural information. Much within his accounts is statistical and a dry read today, yet he also contains lively cameos of many of the places and people he encountered.

For example, Young offers the following account of the poor people of the vicinity of County Louth, Ireland, which is a powerful description for those with ancestors there at this time:

> I made many inquiries concerning the state of the lower classes, and found that in some respects they were in good circumstances,

in others indifferent; they have, generally speaking, such plenty of potatoes as always to command a bellyful; they have flax enough for all their linen, most of them have a cow, and some two, and spin wool enough for their clothes; all a pig, and numbers of poultry, and in general the complete family of cows, calves, hogs, poultry, and children pig together in the cabin; fuel they have in the utmost plenty. Great numbers of families are also supported by the neighbouring lakes, which abound prodigiously with fish. A child with a packthread and a crooked pin will catch perch enough in an hour for the family to live on the whole day... Reverse the medal: they are ill clothed, and make a wretched appearance, and what is worse, are much oppressed by many who make them pay too dear for keeping a cow, horse, etc.... They are much worse treated than the poor in England.

(*Tour in Ireland*, 1776–79)

A half century later William Cobbett made a series of horseback journeys in the 1820s through south England and the English Midlands, recording his observations in *Rural Rides* (1830). As an example of his observations is this one from Sussex:

This village [Billingshurst] is 7 miles from Horsham, and I got here to breakfast about seven o'clock. A very pretty village, and a very nice breakfast, in a very neat little parlour of a very decent public-house. The landlady sent her son to get me some cream, and he was just such a chap as I was at his age, and dressed just in the same sort of way, his main garment being a blue smock-frock, faded from wear, and mended with pieces of new stuff, and, of course, not faded... [with] his nailed shoes, and his clean, plain, and coarse shirt... I was afraid of rain, and got on as fast as I could... However, I had no rain; and got to Petworth, nine miles further, by about ten o'clock.

(*Rural Rides*, 1830)

Someone, somewhere must be related to the son of the landlady of Billingshurst – and many more are related to people born in Billingshurst – and many other places in *Rural Rides* – who would have dressed in this way.

IDEA

Reading tours
William Cobbett's *Rural Rides* is readily available in print, as well as online. It is recommended reading for anyone with ancestors living in the rural south of England in the 1820s. Arthur Young's work is not as readily available, though parts may be found online.

USING MAPS

The British Isles are well provided with old maps. Genealogical information from them is not copious, but they are accessible and well worth considering.

The county boundaries as they existed in your ancestor's time can be crucial to locating records. The old counties are part of the cultural heritage of the British Isles, many having well over a thousand years of identity behind them. The Republic of Ireland has maintained them more or less unchanged, while Northern Ireland has a clear concept of its six counties, though there is also a district structure.

However, the counties of Great Britain have not been so fortunate. The process of change started with the growth of London in the nineteenth and early twentieth centuries which gradually trimmed territory from the surrounding counties. These early changes are minor compared with the wholesale boundary changes of the 1970s, complete with the creation of new counties. Subsequently numerous smaller alterations have distanced the present counties still further from their historic roots. The result is that very often your ancestor didn't live where you think they lived!

TITHE MAPS

The gems among maps for the genealogists are the tithe maps, compiled for England and Wales following the Tithe Commutation Act 1836. These are available both in the National Archives and in local collections, usually CROs in England and the National Library of Wales.

Prior to this Act all farms paid a tithe of their produce to the parish. Strictly this was payable only in kind – as every tenth sheaf of corn, every tenth sheep, even every tenth pail of milk. There were all sorts of difficulties around collection. For starters there was no clarity about whether the parish should collect or whether the farmer should deliver. Then there were all the problems around the practicalities of identifying a tenth of produce. In theory when a field of corn was ready for harvest the farmer should wait for the parish to take their tenth before starting the harvest, risking bad weather damaging the crop.

As a tax, tithes in kind were a system with low rates of collection, high collection costs and an almost endless potential for disputes. They also required the infrastructure of a tithe barn (which was often the biggest barn in the parish) which stored the produce. This was maintained at the parish's expense. Documents called glebe terriers set out the precise customs in a parish and were an effort towards regularizing the system. In practice even before 1836 some parishes had agreed locally that a money payment was to be made in lieu of tithes, calculated as a price per acre. However, many continued with tithes in kind where local agreement could not be reached.

The Tithe Commutation Act converted ('commuted') tithes in kind to money payment using a calculated notional rentable value based on the price of grain. The process required tithe maps to be produced showing every field, and for schedules to be drawn up listing the owner, occupier, the name of the field and the rentable value. The maps themselves are magnificent documents – enormous rolled maps which need a very large desk for consultation. Their size discourages digitization or other repro-duction and the reality is that if you wish to see the maps you usually need to see them in a records office. They are wonderful – though in fairness the maps themselves may not contribute much to your family tree. Of more use for the genealogist are the accompanying schedules – the apportionments – which in effect list all engaged in farming either as a landowner or a tenant.

IDEA

County maps

The *British Atlas* of Pigot & Co (1840) provides useful maps of every county of England and Wales along with commentary on each county. Reprints make this source readily available. Many Victorian and early twentieth-century world atlases have clear county maps of the British Isles. One of the most frequently encountered is Harmsworth's *Universal Atlas and Gazetteer* (1909) – which is a good source also for all the nations of the British Empire.

Old sheet maps tend to be in special collections of libraries and you are most likely to examine what is available than specify a particular map.

Figure 6 Old maps such as this 1896 one for Surrey are a better guide to your ancestors' home than a modern map.

However, if you do order a map a lovely example is The Chart Publishing Company's *Map of England and Wales Showing Railways, Roads and Distances*, published in Oxford, c.1920, and presenting Britain on two large linen-mounted sheets. The Ordnance Survey of Northern Ireland's *Quarter Inch Road Map of Northern Ireland* (Belfast, 1939) is clear for the county boundaries of Northern Ireland.

IDEA

Antique and collectable sheet maps

Old maps from the last decade of the nineteenth century and first half of the twentieth century are readily available in second-hand book-shops or from online sellers. The earliest were intended primarily for cyclists. They provide a visual link to your ancestor's home. Maps to look out for include the following.

▶ Ordnance Survey – this is Great Britain's official map maker, established in 1791. The mass-produced maps from Ordnance Survey (for Great Britain and Ireland) are much more recent, dating from 1914. They are easily found for the 1920s, many with covers which are themselves works of art.

▶ Bartholomew's 'Half-inch to mile' maps of Great Britain were produced in great numbers, and are easily found for the 1930s to 1960s. These are instantly recognizable by their bright blue covers. There are earlier Bartholomew maps – for example, their touring maps of the 1890s which covered England and Wales at four miles to an inch. They also produced maps for the AA.

▶ Other prolific map makers include Johnston's, Philip's (including maps for the RAC), Geographia and Gall & Inglis (mainly Scotland).

Cities are covered both by early street maps and by 'environs' maps which include a radius of so many miles around the city. A major producer of both is Bacon.

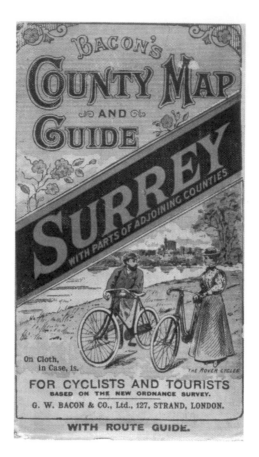

Figure 7 Antiquarian maps can support your understanding of local history.

London maps

London is particularly well served by Map and Plan Collective Online (www.mapco.net), which has a large collection of London maps in high-quality scans, a few of them with some indexing. At the moment there are 73 maps, with more promised.

21

Cluster genealogy and communities

A brick-wall busting technique for the committed researcher is cluster genealogy The basic idea is that social networks of whole communities can be established – extended families, friendships, proximity of accommodation, shared workplace, shared interests, shared faith. Very little work has been done in this area – indeed it is something of a new horizon in genealogy.

USING MILITARY RECORDS IN CLUSTER GENEALOGY

Cluster genealogy is particularly productive with military records. The framework of a military unit is of a group of men who move around together. Where the records relating to one man are missing or have gaps it is often possible to supplement them with records relating to men who served alongside them.

Take, for example, sources for the First World War service of an ancestor. The key document is his medal card, which should be readily available through the National Archives online. However, the information this gives is usually very scant indeed. If you are very lucky service records may also be available – but most have perished.

A cluster genealogy approach is to search the medal card index for all medal cards with a similar regimental number. Numbers were allocated at the time of enlistment and were sequential, so men with similar numbers enlisted at roughly the same time. In the First World War this may even be enlistment on the same day. For example, in the National Archives' search engine replacing the last two digits of your ancestor's number with ** and searching by this plus the regimental name should produce up to a hundred names of men who enlisted at about the same time. Every one of these can then be researched. Some of these may have service records which survive. Some may have died on active service, and therefore be recorded through the Commonwealth War Graves Commission. No single record is likely to be particularly informative but, taken together, these records will show the movements of the men concerned: changes of regiment, postings – the outline of a military career. While there is no one record which alone can indicate your ancestor's movements, if you can identify, say, half a dozen men with regimental numbers above his and half a dozen below (therefore all recruited at about the same time) then you have a group of men who (probably) all trained in the same place, (probably) all moved overseas on the same ship.

EMPLOYING WITNESSES IN CLUSTER GENEALOGY

This cluster genealogy approach has as a hypothesis that witnesses to a document were usually social contacts, frequently friends. For example, two people who witness a man's will will probably be friends, and the families and contacts of these men can in turn be investigated. If on another document one of these witnesses is the witness to the signature of the other witness then a group of three friends has been established. Sometimes it is possible to establish a cluster of even half a dozen friends.

In the earlier centuries of genealogical research most people were part of a tight-knit community – the place where they lived, worked and worshipped. The industrial age changed this for many. Increasingly people can be regarded as a part of three communities. Often home and work were separated, and increasingly people selected a place of worship from among a range of churches. Each of these communities may be investigated as a cluster genealogy project.

THE CHURCH AS SOCIAL CLUSTER

The 1851 religious census (for England, Wales and Scotland but not Ireland) counted the number of people attending every service at every place of worship in Great Britain. Curiously the figures can be hard to interpret because of the double counting caused by people who attended more than one service in the day, either through the same church or different churches. However, the broad-brush result is very clear – more than half of the people who attended a religious service on Sunday, 30 March 1851, were protestant dissenters (i.e. protestants who were not attending the established Church of England). The result caused outrage in the Church of England and much criticism of the circumstances of the census – the Church of England even advanced the view that the heavy rain in many parts of Great Britain on census day had decreased their attendance (though apparently not that of the dissenting churches), while there were allegations that many churches had scheduled a particularly effective preacher for the day in order to boost their attendance.

The religious census does show regional differences which may be of interest to the genealogist. Dissent is highest in Wales, and well above average in the English counties of Northumberland, County Durham and Cornwall. There are also communities where dissent is particularly high, and where a particular dissenting church holds sway.

The 1851 religious census is available through the PRO, with sections available in some CROs and libraries. Many local studies have been based on this census, often at county level, and where these have been published these may be more accessible. If your ancestors were members of an unusual church then it is certainly worth investigating the lives and families of other members of that congregation as these were likely to be part of your ancestors' social group.

Using location in cluster genealogy

Genealogists might benefit from giving thought to the practicalities of travel in the pre-railway age, effectively the period before the 1840s (though the very first passenger railway, the Stockton and Darlington, dates from 1825). Ancestors were part of a geographically restricted community. For most this was at the level of a parish and the immediate neighbourhood; for those who travelled further it was determined by the practicalities of travel.

Horseback

For those with sufficient wealth to afford a horse, this was the simplest and most flexible manner of travel. Speeds were slow. In the fourteenth century Chaucer's Canterbury Pilgrims are described as taking two days to ride the sixty miles from London to Canterbury. On the eve of the railway age improved roads permitted a journey of this length to be managed in a single summer's day with the maximum hours of daylight and good weather conditions, though a winter's journey would still have been two days. Issues around the stabling and maintenance of a horse often discouraged the use of a horse for long-distance journeys. People in this social class frequently travelled widely in their life, and may have married someone from a different part of the country. Sometimes it is possible to find families with property or other interests in two or more distinct locations, and travel of all family members between these two locations is something to look out for.

Coach

Travel in a private coach was only for the very wealthy, while stagecoach travel still required a level of income above that of labourers or most involved in trade. While stagecoaches certainly existed in the sixteenth century, and private coaches somewhat earlier, it was really only from the mid-eighteenth century that there was a network of roads available to support their wide-spread use. This is the age of the turnpike, a network of around 30,000 miles of road maintained by private companies to government-set standards and funded by tolls. However, even on the turnpikes speeds were slow. Towards the end of the eighteenth century London to Bristol could be managed in a scheduled 17 hours – a time then considered fast and often in reality 24 hours – while the London to Holyhead road (for ships to Dublin) took around 45 hours. Speeds were typically five to six miles per hour. There were many improvements to roads in the early nineteenth century, with speeds rising to nine or even ten miles per hour (and London to Holyhead reduced on some runs to a mere 27 hours!) The most travelled stagecoach routes were those that radiated out from London.

For the genealogist it is worth remembering that people tended to move where the turnpikes ran, and looking at a turnpike map can help understand eighteenth-century movements. The turnpike network was centred on London, and it is from this time that London grows rapidly.

On foot

Prior to the mid-eighteenth century the reality was that most people walked, and even after the mid-eighteenth century all but the wealthy walked. People carried their belongings on their back or pulled them in a two-wheeled handcart – and they walked from end to end of the country.

Figure 8 'Waiting for the Train': this 1864 painting by Erskine Nicol evokes the spirit of migration by train in the British Isles.

Pre-railway age migration

The genealogical implications for pre-railway age migrations include the following.

- Women travelled far less than men. Prior to the stagecoach age, women's migration was unusual. When it is found it is most likely to be in the context of a newly married couple moving to an area of greater economic opportunity, and the image of a young couple pulling a handcart may well be correct.

- Where women are found travelling during the stagecoach age it may suggest a degree of family affluence.

- Migrations were often along roads served by stagecoaches. This is particularly pronounced along some of the well-established routes, including the London to Edinburgh Great North Road. London to York took in excess of 30 hours; York to Edinburgh again in excess of 30 hours; yet this was a migration trunk route.

- Most people never travelled more than six miles from their home. For most the world was their parish and the nearest market town, and perhaps some neighbouring parishes. The most common migration (particularly for women) was to the nearest market town.

- Sea routes played a significant part in migrations, leading to some unexpected migration routes. South Wales and north Devon were a short distance over the Bristol Channel, leading to many links between Cardiff and the ports of north Devon. The Antrim glens of Ireland were in many respects closer to southwest Scotland than to the hinterland of Ireland.

Cluster genealogy can help to understand the flows within migration. While each individual movement is unique to the person undertaking it, within communities there are flows which are regular and may be described.

EXPLORING NINETEENTH-CENTURY MIGRATIONS

The population of many British Isles rural areas peaked around 1841; from 1871 many rural areas saw significant depopulation. The nineteenth century transformed the British Isles from a land of villages to a land of towns and cities.

The key document for understanding nineteenth-century migrations in the British Isles is a statistician's conclusions published in the 1885 *Journal of the Royal Statistical Society* (E. G. Ravenstein's 'The laws of migration'). Here are set out the following concepts.

- Most migrants are adults and unmarried.

- Most migrants travel only a short distance, mostly within a county.

- Many longer migrations are a series of short-distance migrations.

- The few migrants who go long distances generally go to a major centre of commerce or industry, in effect to a big city.

- Most migrants come from rural districts, not from towns.

- There are more women migrants than men, especially within a county.

- Longer migrations are more often made by men than women.

■   The reason for migration is usually for employment.

For the genealogist these laws do provide some clues. Most important is the concept that a Victorian couple are unlikely to marry then migrate – rather, migration usually takes place prior to marriage. Typically the location where a couple marry is the vicinity where they will raise their family and live out their lives. However, in these cases the marriage record rarely gives information of the real place of origin of either; rather, the parish or address given is where they have been living prior to the marriage, but after a migration. When a nineteenth-century migration is suspected the probabilities in Table 2 may be examined.

Table 2. Possible reasons for nineteenth-century migration

	Living in town	Living in city
Man	Probably born there	Probably long-distance migrant from rural area outside the county
Woman	Probably short-distance migrant from rural area in the county	Probably born there

A feature of nineteenth-century migrations in the British Isles is that they began to include extended families. Perhaps a single member would migrate, and then a number of family members – unmarried brothers and sisters – follow in the footsteps of the first migrant. These migrations may include also an older generation moving with their children.

Figure 9 A 1902 sketch of Trafalgar Square and St Martin-in-the-Fields by Mortimer Menpes.

RELIGION AND MIGRATION

Religion has only rarely been a motive for migration in the British Isles. It has, however, been a factor behind some international migrations.

Roman Catholics on occasions fled a country that made their religion illegal. From the late sixteenth century, migrations to the European continent (mainly France) took place, though in small numbers and mainly as an upper-class phenomenon. Migration by Roman Catholics in the eighteenth century and early nineteenth century to the New World may have had a religious dimension, but was usually primarily economic in its motivation.

The major religious migrations are protestant. From the *Mayflower* Pilgrim Fathers (1620) onwards many protestant dissenters left the British Isles for the New World – perhaps 20,000 in just the two decades following the *Mayflower*. These settlers often had their faith as a primary reason for migration. An example is the migration of Quakers in the late seventeenth century: indeed the state of Pennsylvania takes its name from its Quaker founder, William Penn, and many of the settlers from the 1680s and 1690s were Quakers. At just the time the Quakers were fleeing from Britain another protestant group, the Huguenots, were taking refuge in Britain. The French king Louis XIV in 1685 declared the protestant faith to be illegal, prompting around 60,000 protestant refugees – the Huguenots – to make their homes in Britain. Of the 60,000 Huguenots most settled in London and the English Home Counties, and many worked as weavers. Smaller numbers settled in Bristol, Plymouth and in Ulster, this last group creating the Ulster linen industry which continues today.

IDEA

Huguenot ancestors

Suspected Huguenot ancestry can be investigated – assuming you have traced a line back to the late seventeenth and early eighteenth centuries. Almost all original records of Huguenots are now in the National Archives. Additionally most are published, and the printed versions are both easier to access and quicker to search. Many Huguenot families can be traced back to their French roots. The standard guide is *Les Familles Protestantes en France* by Gildas Bernard (1987, Paris, Archives Nationales).

22

Military records

The records of the armed forces are an enormous body of material which has the potential to break through brick walls. However, using these records has frustrations.

Prior to 1872 records are arranged by regiment. In order to find an ancestor you need to know which regiment he was in – and without this information you really cannot start. You also need to know or at least suspect that an ancestor was even in a regiment. Many men, particularly the younger sons of families, indeed spent a time in the armed forces. You may perhaps suspect that this is the case when a man makes a first marriage in his mid-thirties – but it is a long road from a suspicion to finding a record.

COUNTY REGIMENTS

County affiliations are found from 1782, though regimental recruitment areas had little to do with these counties. True county regiments with a local affiliation are from 1881, when regiments had a recruitment area which at least roughly corresponded with the counties they were named after. This might give a starting point. However, the process is far from simple. Recruitment areas overlapped – especially in London – while a man might choose to serve in a regiment that his father had served in. Regiments were sometimes garrisoned in areas remote from their origin but would recruit men from the area where they were garrisoned.

TRACING REGIMENT MOVEMENTS

Regiments were frequently divided into two battalions, one serving overseas and one stationed in the UK ready to relieve the overseas battalion. The campaigns and battles an ancestor might have been involved in therefore depend on the battalion he served in as much as the regiment. In times of war the number of battalions was increased – with an enormous increase for most regiments during the First World War. In order to understand an ancestor's regimental movements it is essential to look at battalion as well as regiment.

RANKS

A soldier enlisting could hope to progress through merit through the categories of non-commissioned officers and other ranks:

- private;
- lance corporal;
- corporal;
- sergeant;
- staff sergeant;
- sergeant major;
- warrant officer 2nd class;
- warrant officer 1st class.

The contrast is with commissioned officers, most of whom in the period prior to 1871 would have bought their commission:

- 2nd lieutenant;
- lieutenant;
- captain;
- major;
- lieutenant colonel;
- colonel;
- brigadier;
- major general;
- lieutenant general;
- general;
- field marshal.

Commissioned officers' careers can usually be tracked through the pages of the *London Gazette* and supplemented by military records – in effect, the *London Gazette* shows you where to look.

IDEA

Military photographs

Identifying a regiment and dating a photograph from a uniform is not easy but can be done. Points to look at include the following.

▶ Photographs of men in uniform which include a visible badge (cap, collar or belt) will reveal a regiment. However, for this you do need a clear image of the badge and, while a few photographs do have the required resolution, most don't. Usually the most that can be got from a cap badge in a photograph is confirmation that it is consistent with the general shape of the cap badge of a suspected regiment.

▶ Cap badges were introduced in 1881 along with reform of the county affiliation of regiments. The existence or otherwise of a cap badge is therefore a dating feature. Collar badges were introduced in 1874 for other ranks, 1881 for officers, and are frequently very similar to the cap badges. They are smaller and usually even less visible than the cap badges.

▶ Unfortunately the uniforms alone are frequently not helpful in identifying a regiment. There was much overlap, while uniforms show frequent changes and a level of complexity which taxes even the specialists. For example, the Glengarry Cap was introduced in 1874 and by 1880 had become commonplace in British regiments, before going out of fashion in all but some Scots regiments. Sometimes there are uniform giveaways. For example, the Guards Division regiments have distinctive button spacing on their red tunics:
   – Grenadier Guards: single;
   – Coldstream Guards: pairs;
   – Scots Guards: threes;
   – Irish Guards: fours;
   – Welsh Guards: fives.

▶ Interpreting stripes can be problematic. Rank badges are on the upper arm or right cuff. Long-service stripes are worn on the left arm just above the cuff (one for two years, two for six years, three for twelve years and four for eighteen years). Vertical lines on the left cuff are wound stripes. During the First World War the army used overseas service stripes (one per year) worn on the right arm.

IDEA

Regiments' records
Regiments do not (generally) hold records of individual soldiers but they do hold a range of information including muster rolls, pay lists, diaries and photographs, and they may well additionally have a regimental museum. There can be difficulties in finding just what is preserved as collections are frequently poorly indexed, while access to researchers is usually limited – indeed the normal approach is for the genealogist to take the services of a volunteer researcher in return for a donation.

Figure 10 A Scots Guard may be identified by his tunic buttons in groups of three – far more visible than the cap badge in this 1912 photograph.

The websites of regiments vary enormously in their interest to genealogists. One that is excellent is that of the Gloucestershire Regiment (Glosters) (www.glosters.org.uk). This site allows a search through an index of their nineteenth-century and First World War records. It is an example of the sort of resource genealogists would love to see for every regiment.

IDEA

Soldiers' families
Many soldiers were married. The life of their children may be explored through Army Children (www.archhistory.co.uk).

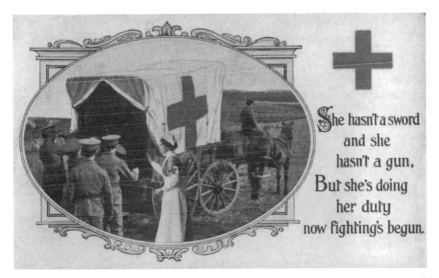

She hasn't a sword
and she
hasn't a gun,
But she's doing
her duty
now fighting's begun.

Figure 11 Women also saw service overseas in wars, as these First World War VAD nurses.

IDEA

Searching for medals
Up to and including the First World War, UK medals were issued with the name of the bearer engraved around them. There is a chance of

being reunited with the medals of an ancestor through the website www.medaltracker.com, a commercial service which lists medals for sale by name.

Chelsea Pensioner records

Discharge records of men who received a pension are available 1760–1913 through the collection of the Royal Hospital, Chelsea – and from 1883 these include the discharge papers additionally of those who did not receive a pension.

Figure 12 The Last Muster, Sunday at the Royal Hospital, Chelsea. This 1875 picture by Sir Herbert von Herkomer appears to show the death of a Chelsea pensioner sitting at the end of the second row.

23

Occupational records

One snippet of information usually found about an ancestor is their occupation. Investigation of a job can add depth to the picture of an ancestor.

INVESTIGATING RURAL OCCUPATIONS

Traditionally, the English rural scene was dominated by the occupations of yeoman, husbandman and cottager. Farmer was not usually used until the nineteenth century (the older meaning of the word is a completely different occupation, that of tax collector).

Yeoman, husbandman and cottager

A yeoman was traditionally a man with an income of 40 shillings or more per year (and thus entitled to vote). The yeoman class existed from at least the twelfth century (when an income of 40 shillings p.a. equated to around 40 acres of land) until well into the nineteenth century when the widening of the franchise made the concept of yeoman less meaningful. The yeoman class were the prestigious members of a local community, but below the class of gentleman, though frequently the distinction between yeoman and gentleman was blurred. A husbandman had a lower annual income (and therefore traditionally did not have a vote). Cottager was the occupation of someone living in a tied cottage – one of the occupations that came to be known as 'agricultural labourer'.

Agricultural labourer

The term 'agricultural labourer' – usually recorded simply as 'Ag Lab' – was created specifically for the 1841 census. It is an umbrella term for a variety of occupations with significant differences in their character. It is always worth while trying to go beneath the term 'ag lab' and find out what was the real occupation. Some of the major types are as follows.

■ Farm servants: these are boys or young men who usually resided at the farm and who were contracted to work for one year. On a census they show up in the farmer's household. Frequently their role was much the same as that of a farmer's son and they tended to be employed when the farmer did not have sons of an appropriate age. Very often they were relatives, perhaps a nephew, grandson or cousin of the farmer.

■ Servants of husbandry: these were typically men hired at an annual hiring fair and contracted to work for a year. They were paid a wage, plus board and lodging and, like the farm servants, often lived in the farmer's home, but they tended to be older than the farm servants and were much less likely to be a relative. Often they had a specific role – shepherd or plough-man or cow-hand, for example – but regrettably the census and BMD often do not record this. They were a relatively mobile group in society.

■ Cottager: typically a married man who lived with his family in a cottage on or close to the farm (for which rent was usually paid) and receiving a wage in return for fixed hours of labour.

On the census such families can be identified because the head of the household is an 'ag lab' with wife and children.

- Men in rural occupations not classified as husbandman, yeoman or gentleman or by another precise title. For example, men living on their son's farm (and presumably effectively retired) may be labelled 'ag lab'.

Figure 13 The home of an English cottager, as depicted by Mortimer Menpes.

In the mid-nineteenth century agricultural labourers received surprisingly variable wages in different parts of the country. Some of the highest wages were in Yorkshire (in 1851 in the region of 11–14 shillings a week), while many southern counties of England and much of Scotland saw agricultural labourers receiving around 7 shillings a week. The variation reflects the existence of alternative employment in the industrial cities of the north of England and the consequent relative scarcity of farm workers in that area. Many agricultural labourers – certainly those on 7 shillings a week – were scarcely able to feed themselves and their families, but it is an oversimplification to see all agricultural labourers as living in a state of poverty. Many cottagers in the nineteenth century (and perhaps most in pre-industrial Britain) had a simple but adequate home, fixed hours of labour and benefited from up to half an acre of allotment around their cottage used to grow vegetables and (particularly in the south of England) to keep a pig. Agricultural labourer can reflect a life of extreme toil, but the same term can also be applied to a comfortable lifestyle.

The move away from the land was intensified by the 'agricultural depression' of the 1870s and the poor performance of agriculture for the remainder of the nineteenth century. Particularly affected was arable farming, which faced American cereal which was cheaper than that grown at home. Livestock farming experienced fewer problems but could not escape the disruption of the countryside caused by the agricultural depression.

For a better understanding of the ubiquitous occupation 'ag lab' a key source is the book *My Ancestor was an Agricultural Labourer*, Ian H. Waller (Society of Genealogists, 2008).

IDEA

Exploring rural occupations
Numerous museums of rural life are found throughout the British Isles, offering a glimpse into the lifestyles of ancestors working in the country. One of the biggest is the Museum of English Rural Life, founded by the University of Reading (www.ruralhistory.org), which offers collections including archives, photographs and books.

RESEARCHING SERVANTS

In 1851 around three quarters of a million women were employed as servants, around one in nine of the adult women in the UK. As with 'ag lab', 'servant' was something of a catch-all occupation. Fortunately the census and BMD often record the type of servant, very useful for understanding what job they actually did. The numbers employed as servants peaked around the time of the 1891 census when around a third of women of working age were in domestic service. Additionally many daughters of households living at home and with no occupation recorded on the census were in effect doing the job of a domestic servant.

The concept of daughters living at home being *de facto* domestic servants indicates how the role was perceived. It was not a job with a contract and regular working hours but, rather, one where women worked all hours and all days to support the life of a household. When a household did not have a daughter of appropriate age at home then a domestic servant was sought. Middle-class families typically employed one to three servants. For the genealogist it is important to note that very many women in domestic service in middle-class homes were working for a relative, as the extended family was frequently the grapevine through which households found their domestic servants and through which women in need of employment sought work.

The foundation role for the servant in small households was that of the maid-of-all-work or general servant. On their role Mrs Beeton's *Book of Household Management* (1861) comments: 'the mistress's commands are the measure of the Maid-of-all-Work's duties', while accounts indicate that working days were frequently sixteen hours, and the labour unrelenting.

The servant's lifestyle was different in the Victorian and Georgian country houses, which frequently constituted a whole community under one roof. Typically a country house might employ one to two dozen indoor servants and a similar number of outdoor servants.

Men servants

Men servants are far less numerous than women, and very few men servants were employed indoors. Only the biggest households had the indoor roles of butler, footman or a gentleman's valet. Usually men were employed outdoors. They are usually described by their speciality, so not as servant but rather as gardener or groom or coachman or gamekeeper or some similar, precise role. While women tended to see their time as a servant as a short-term occupation, for many men their employment was perceived as a lifelong vocation.

IDEA

Mrs Beeton
The key book on household management – effectively the management of servants – is that published by Mrs Beeton (Isabella Mary Mayson) in 1861. Its long title indicates its scope: *The Book of Household Management Comprising Information for the Mistress, Housekeeper, Cook, Kitchen-maid, Butler, Footman, Coachman, Valet, Upper and Under House-maids, Lady's-maid, Maid-of-all-work, Laundry-maid, Nurse and Nurse-maid, Monthly Wet and Sick Nurses, etc. etc. – also Sanitary, Medical, & Legal Memoranda: with a History of the Origin, Properties, and Uses of all Things Connected with Home Life and Comfort.* It is a superb source for information about nineteenth-century servants' duties.

The book has been reprinted very many times and is readily available both in libraries and bookshops. It is also available online at www.mrsbeeton.com.

IDEA

Servants as poor relations
If your ancestors employed servants or were domestic servants, investigate the families of the employer and of all servants, for possible relationship. Servants were frequently the poor relations of middle-class employers.

IDEA

Country-house servants
Country-house servants are unlikely to be related to the employer. However, two or more servants from a single family may be employed at the same country house, and marriages between servants are relatively common. Consider the possibility that some of the servants employed alongside your ancestor may be relatives.

Many country house servants spent their career with one employer. This might include moving home with that employer, or moving between different homes owned by the employer. Investigating the life of the employer might provide some hints to servants' movements.

WOMEN'S LABOUR

As an alternative to employment as servants, women were also engaged in a variety of home industries. The most common were:

- dressmaking;

- glove making;

- lace making;

- straw-plaiting;

- box making;

- carding (preparing wool for spinning);

- chain making;

- button making;

- nail making.

Some of these home industries were regional – for example, straw-plaiting is particularly associated with Bedfordshire and neighbouring counties as a wheat variety that produced an appropriate straw was grown there.

Wages varied enormously. They often reflected the skill of the individual home-worker and – contrary to expectation – could sometimes be good. Indeed many in the early nineteenth century were concerned that the wages paid to women were so high that women were becoming the main earner in a household, allowing men to be lazy!

IDEA

Women home-workers
Records of specific workers in these industries are scant. A fruitful source of context is to search for all examples of a particular occupation within a particular town on a given census. This cluster genealogy approach may show patterns of place of residence, age and marital condition.

Figure 14 A pieman, 1884 – a typical urban occupation of the age.

RESEARCHING INDUSTRIAL OCCUPATIONS

Records are typically in CROs or local studies centres at libraries. In addition to the records created by the employers there may also be trades union records.

Figure 15 The railways were one of the largest employers of the late Victorian age. These porters are shown around 1885.

Railway

Railway records of employees are a remarkable source. From the Railway Act 1844 to the 1947 nationalization of the railways they provide a copious source of information.

There is no standardization for railway staff records. Around a thousand railway companies operated in the British Isles during the century leading up to nationalization and every company had its own system of record keeping. Many of the records are extensive. A staff record might include date of birth, address, next of kin, previous occupation, a note of military service at any time, promotions, commendations, punishments, sickness payments, date of retirement, pension received, date of death – a level of detail for a life paralleled by few other classes of records. Additionally there may well be trades union membership records.

IDEA

Weird and wonderful records
Sometimes the most amazing collections can exist – and if they do then use them. For example, the Local Studies Centre in Brighton contains a resource which may well be unique. This is a collection of twelve, closely written notebooks compiled by H. E. S. Simmons listing the landlords of around 600 Brighton pubs in the period 1848–1936 or thereabouts – around 10,000 landlords. With this resource it is relatively quick to identify a Brighton pub landlord with their dates of tenure.

PROFESSIONAL OCCUPATIONS

Employment in the professions has generated documentation. Usually these occupations required a university degree, which means a record in the alumni listing of the appropriate university. Additionally the profession will have records ranging from newspaper coverage to specific archives. For example, the Anglican clergy are one of the easiest groups to trace, largely thanks to a magnificent database from the Church of England (www.theclergydatabase.org.uk).

Freemasonry

Records of Freemasons and other fraternal societies are very much a new frontier of genealogical research, yet they may come to be a fruitful source.

Towards the end of the nineteenth century most professional men were members of a fraternal society. Typically they made a regular contribution to the society and received benefits which might include funeral costs or support for their widows and children. The Freemasons were the biggest group, but there were many others.

Identifying membership is often problematic. Some of the most promising sources are photographs of men in fraternal regalia, which can often be identified. Notices of funerals may include information about fraternal links (especially if the fraternal organization was funding it), while headstones sometimes include Masonic symbols.

The mottos of some major fraternal organizations are:

- Buffaloes: philanthropy, conviviality, integrity;

- Druids: united to assist;

- Foresters: unitas, benevolentia, concordia;

- Oddfellows: amicitia, amor et veritas;

- Rechabites: peace and plenty – the rewards of temperance.

24

Ireland: problems and inspiration

Irish research has difficulties not faced in England, and more extreme than those faced in Wales and Scotland. They can be summarized under three headings.

■ Many records which exist in England never existed in Ireland.

■ Many records which once existed in Ireland have been destroyed.

■ The indexing of Irish records is frequently less good than for many comparable records elsewhere.

RECORDS THAT NEVER EXISTED

That records never existed is a reality that the Irish researcher has to take on board. It is hard to take most Irish family lines back beyond the late eighteenth century. This is because parish registers that were kept by the Church of England and other protestant churches in Great Britain are not directly paralleled by the records of the Roman Catholic church in Ireland – and the majority of people in Ireland were Roman Catholic. That said, records relating to the Church of Ireland and to protestants in Ireland were compiled in much the same way as in England (though their preservation is another matter).

To have any real chance of tracing an Irish line through the eighteenth century and earlier that line needs to be protestant and relatively affluent – and the two very often went together in Ireland. This is not wholly dissimilar to the position of researchers of English lines, though it is more extreme. Those researching English families much before the late eighteenth century will find it hard to make much progress with lines that were poor – rather, it is the yeoman farmers and gentlemen who trace best – and will also find that Roman Catholic records are more problematic than those of the Church of England.

RECORDS DESTROYED

The big destruction of Irish records came in 1922 during the Irish Civil War when the Public Record Office of Ireland at the Four Courts, Dublin, was destroyed. As well as most nineteenth-

Figure 16 Dublin's Four Courts, the scene of the 1922 fire which destroyed many of Ireland's archives.

century census returns the destruction consumed pre-1858 wills and administrations, and about half of the Church of Ireland parish registers, along with a mass of documents going back almost a thousand years. This is a terrible loss of a nation's cultural heritage.

RECORDS NOT INDEXED

Much of the indexing of parish registers for the British Isles has been carried out by the Church of Jesus Christ of Latter Day Saints (Mormons). The Roman Catholic church has reservations about the use made of parish registers by this group – their unease is around the Mormon practice of posthumous baptism of relatives of Mormons into the Mormon faith, something which is considered to be an aberrant practice of an heretical group. As a result many Roman Catholic church registers have not been made available to the Mormons, including most of those for Ireland.

However, the Roman Catholic church's decision to restrict access to the Mormons is only practical if access is severely restricted. As a consequence there has been a reluctance to make the registers available in a format which the Mormons could easily access – for example, by publication of page scans of transcription. Frequently access to Roman Catholic church records in Ireland is still only through the physical register, whether at the church or through the local record offices. These sources are almost always un-indexed. The process of searching is very slow for the researcher.

IS THERE ANY GOOD NEWS?

It is very easy to lament what is not available. That Ireland should once have had one of the most extensive national archives of any nation and for this to have been lost is tantalizing. An effect has been that Irish genealogists have been more inventive in using other records – both records unique to Ireland and records which exist elsewhere in the British Isles but have been little used.

Griffith's valuations (1830s–1860s)

Griffith's valuations have no counterpart outside Ireland. These boundary surveys and land valuations were carried out under the direction of Richard John Griffith. Each county has different dates for the start and the end of the survey, while the actual publication of the results was some years later, starting in 1847. They provide extensive information both about landowners and those renting the land. The pattern of land use in Ireland was that land was divided and subdivided into tiny plots, with the great majority of families renting their own plot or plots – the system contrasts markedly with England, Wales and much of Scotland where a class of agricultural labourers neither owned nor rented land.

Griffith's valuations are often described by genealogists as a 'census substitute'. They are not as useful as census returns – but they are better than nothing. They are available online and for free, and are supported by an excellent search engine (www.ask aboutireland.ie/griffith-valuation).

Return of land owners (1876)

Another 'census substitute' for Ireland is the return of land owners. As with Griffith's valuations, most Irish families are named in the return – but unlike Griffith's valuations this is a survey of the whole British Isles. It records rental incomes with the names of both the owners and occupiers of land of one acre or more. It is sometimes nicknamed the 'Second Domesday Book'.

Boards charged with making the returns were established in 1872. Returns were made for England and Wales (excluding London) in 1873, Scotland in 1874 and Ireland in 1876.

IDEA

Return of land owners as a British Isles resource
If you are researching an Irish family then this is an essential document. If your family is elsewhere in the British Isles these returns are, none the less, interesting and may supplement the census information. Some English and Welsh returns are recorded online available through UK Genealogy Archives. Welsh, Scottish and Irish returns are available through www.cefnpennar.com/1873index.htm.

Information is brief. For example, the register for Cardiganshire records that Evans, William Jones of Llandovery had land of 69A 2R 20P with a gross estimated rental value of f45 9s.

The measures used are the traditional ones of acre (A), rood (R) and square pole (P):

▶ an acre is 1/640th of a square mile;

▶ a rood is a ploughing strip 220 yards long (1 furlong) and 5½ yards wide. There are four roods to an acre;

▶ a square pole is 30¼ square yards – 40 square poles comprise one rood, or 160 square poles comprise one acre.

Working with this system of land measure does wonders for your arithmetic!

25

International genealogy

Many genealogy brick walls are around international genealogy. The British Isles has three major sorts of international genealogical links:

- migration from the British Isles to America or to nations of the British Empire or Commonwealth;

- migration to the British Isles. Prior to the Second World War this is usually from the Continent of Europe;

- travel by British families, primarily through the British Empire but also to the Continent of Europe.

A common international brick wall is a collateral relative who was born and married in the British Isles, then that relative and their family appear to vanish. Often this is because of emigration, but there are challenges in finding where the relative went and in picking up their family in the new location. Immigration into the British Isles may be traceable because census records give a place of birth, or may well have frustrations. Hardest to trace is often the travel people made through their lives.

INVESTIGATING BRITISH EMPIRE RECORDS

A starting point for all British Empire genealogy is records held in the British Isles. These are copious, ranging from BMD to military records with numerous special collections. Additionally the newspapers of the British Isles reported news from throughout the Empire, while English-language newspapers from overseas are usually available through the British Library.

Records overseas are frequently copious, often as copious as those in the UK, as the British system was exported throughout the Empire. They are often difficult to access and difficult to search. Researchers who have had success with British Empire records overseas seem for the most part to have used the services of professional researchers in the locality who have familiarity with the records available and the appropriate language skills.

EUROPE

The records of the European Continent are extensive – in many cases as or even more prolific than those of the British Isles. However, with few exceptions, they are far less accessible. The continental system is overwhelmingly one of local preservation with little in the way of centralized indexes so, unless you know the precise area in which to search, you may well encounter problems. Often the UK records don't make the transition to continental records easy. For example, the UK census returns record (from 1851) parish of birth of individuals from the home country, but when someone is born in Germany (for example) they record just 'Germany'. This creates a major problem as there is no centralization for German records.

In general the nations of Europe have a parish register system very much on the lines of the British Isles. However, the preservation of older records is in general much less good than in England. Most European nations have a transition from churches recording vital events to civil registration but, whereas the nations of the UK have centralized indexes (England and Wales, Scotland and Ireland), the European civil records are mostly local systems. Additionally not all nations have the level of access that British Isles genealogists have become accustomed to. For example, in Switzerland access to vital records is primarily for officials and, while it is possible (and reasonably straightforward) for individuals to get access, the system does require that permission be granted.

Broad hints in the use of continental European records as they affect British Isles genealogists include the following.

France:

- The French Revolution started in 1792 a process of recording all births, marriages and deaths through the *mairie* (town hall), a process which continues. Pre-1792 parish registers were deposited with the *mairie*. French genealogical records are dominated by the local preservation in the *mairie* itself, in local libraries and in local record offices. While centralized indexes are being produced they do not replace the essential localism. If you are researching family connections with France your starting point is the local area and the particular records preserved for that area.

- Many French ancestors of British people are Huguenots, whose records are considered elsewhere (page 125).

- The French Revolution brought French aristocrats and their families to Britain. Records of French armorial families can be found through the *Bibliothèque nationale*. When the records are in the form of printed books these can usually be accessed through the Inter-library Loan system. A useful starting point is that library's catalogue at www.bnf.fr.

Germany:

■ German unification dates from 1871. In 1814 (after the Congress of Vienna) the German Confederation consisted of 39 sovereign states. As a consequence genealogical records differ from area to area and are almost all preserved locally. Genealogists need to know a region in order to start searching, yet UK records of migrants frustratingly usually just record 'Germany'.

■ The majority of German ancestry in the UK is from German Jews who migrated in considerable numbers from 1848 onwards. If you are researching a German surname or an ancestor from Germany it is most likely that that person was Jewish, even if they did not subsequently practise their faith in the UK. It is therefore sensible to examine Jewish records available in the UK, which are generally well indexed and accessible.

Austro-Hungarian Empire:

■ Parish registers are extensive; civil registration came late to Austro-Hungary. In the nations of the former eastern Europe there are significant issues around both the cataloguing of collections and access. While records may well exist there can be problems in locating them.

■ Many people from the Austro-Hungarian Empire migrating to the UK were Jews and, as with German ancestors, it makes sense to start with UK Jewish records, even if Jewish ancestry is not suspected.

Holland:

■ The system is that every municipality (about 1,000) keeps its own BMD records. There is some duplication by provinces, but little or no centralization.

■ English and Scottish merchants trading with Holland frequently concluded contracts in Holland, and many of these records have survived, particularly linked with Rotterdam. The records are catalogued by the name of the notary who prepared the document. Indexes are coming into existence, and this area may well become useful for British Isles genealogists.

Norway:

■ Emigrant lists were compiled by local police from the 1860s listing people emigrating from Norway. Most went to the USA but a few did migrate to the British Isles. The records have been moved to regional archive offices. For example, the Oslo Regional Archive Office has lists of emigrants by White Star Line, 1883–1923. The web gateway to Norwegian archives is www.arkivverket.no.

Spain:

■ Civil registration came to Spain in 1870. Earlier church registers are now generally in cathedral archives. As well as baptisms, marriages and burials they include confirmation records.

Italy:

■ Church registers are extensive (especially subsequent to the Council of Trent, 1563). Most are in *Archivio di Stato*, found in every major town.

■ Notarial records are mostly in the *Archivio Centrale dello Stato* in Rome (www.acs.beniculturali.it).

IDEA

Ellis Island records

For any collateral relative who simply vanishes, it is worth considering the possibility of emigration. The problem of course is in knowing where to start looking. As with all genealogical problems start with what is easily and cheaply available. In this case start with the remarkable and free database of passengers arriving at New York, many of them migrants. The site can be searched at www.ellisisland.org.

IDEA

Ship records

Ancestors On Board (www.ancestorsonboard.com) has been produced by Findmypast.co.uk, in association with the National Archives, and it gives the outward-bound passengers on ships leaving the UK from the

1890s to the 1960s – and including a few earlier records. The database is of everyone travelling, so it picks up emigrants as well as business-men, soldiers and diplomats.

26

Photographs

Family photographs present two sorts of brick walls. The first is around finding them. If you have them, you have a super genealogical asset – if you don't, the opportunities for locating them may not be obvious but there are some. The second sort of brick wall is around interpreting those photographs you have.

FINDING PHOTOGRAPHS

The following are among the key sources for finding photographs.

- Known relatives: probably one or more of your relatives have photographs relating to your ancestors – ask!

- Distant relatives found online: the ease of transmission of scanned photographs means that most are happy to share.

- Google: it can be as simple as entering a name and finding an image. You need an unusual full name (with speech marks around it) entered as a Google image search. No, it doesn't happen often, but it does happen.

- Victoria and Albert Museum: several collections are worth both searching and browsing, including a marvellous archive of wedding photographs at www.vam.ac.uk/things-to-do/wedding-fashion/home.

- National Portrait Gallery: a surprisingly large cross-section of British people have their image preserved through the NPG (www.npg.org.uk), often in the form of photographs or paintings that are not on display in the gallery. The collection is well indexed.

- National archives: photographic collections are a fast-growing area.

- Local studies centres: most have photographic resources which they are making available.

In addition to these sources there is a growing industry around commercial photograph sources for genealogists. This area is very much in its infancy but is an exciting new development. For example, a commercial company may collect photographs of soldiers of the First World War and index them by name and regiment. The photographs are available for purchase. At the moment only a tiny proportion of soldiers have been covered in this way, but it is a growing source.

DATING PHOTOGRAPHS

This is a key piece of information for contextualizing a photograph, and sometimes for identifying individuals in the photo. There are several methods for dating a photo – and dating should, where possible, use more than one method. These are:

- the date the photographic studio was trading;
- the type of photograph;
- the costume shown; and
- the event.

Dating the studio

From the 1860s to the early 1900s many photographs have the name of the photographic studio either on the front or the back. Most studios were short lived, and most studios had entries in trade directories. Usually reference to trade directories can determine when the studio was in business and therefore indicate a date. For London photographic studios there is a website (www.photolondon.org.uk) which gives information on the date of pre-1901 studios.

Photographic studios did not generally keep records of their work. Even in those cases where you have the name of a studio and a reference number for a picture it is most unlikely that you will be able to trace any information about that picture.

Dating the type of photograph

The physical form of photographs has changed continually through the age of the photograph. It is practical to date a photograph by comparison with other photographs of a known date – either that you have or which may be found on the Internet. Broad guidelines on type are as follows.

■ Daguerreotype (1839–50s), the first commercial photograph. The image is produced on a surface of highly polished silver on a copper plate treated with iodine and developed using mercury vapour. The silver was expensive, the mercury vapour dangerous and the exposure time at first around 10 minutes, though later reduced to under 2 minutes. Such photographs are rare items today.

■ Ambrotype (1854–mid-1860s), the first widely available photograph. This is a negative image on glass on a black background. The background makes the whites black, while the greys remain grey. The resulting image is therefore black and grey and with right and left reversed (so rings are on the wrong hand and clothes button the wrong way). Most ambrotypes are cased, usually with a gold-coloured frame made of the alloy pinchbeck. Most do not include the name of the photographer.

- *Carte de visite* (1850s–1890s) is the first commercial photograph on paper, made by exposing a negative and therefore capable of duplication. The technology stems from the Fox Talbot paper process announced in 1839 (within days of the Daguerreotype) but which was not then commercial. The paper uses a surface of albumen (egg white) and silver nitrate. Typically photographs are 3¼ inches × 2¼ inches, mounted on a card and with a studio name clearly displayed. The name was invented in Britain to indicate that such photographs might be used in lieu of the visiting card, though in fact few of the many people who had *cartes de visite* taken would have been in a social class to require visiting cards.

- Cabinet prints (mostly 1880s and 1890s) are like *cartes de visite* in that they use a negative and are printed on albumen paper, but a little larger (frequently 4 × 5½ inches) and mostly mounted on board. The studio name is usually displayed.

- Tintype (1856–1890s) is the cheapest form of Victorian photograph. A single photographic plate was exposed section by section to take a dozen or more photographs, then the plate was developed within the camera and cut up to separate the photographs. The process was very common at fairs. A 'gem tintype' is a 1 inch × 1½ inch photograph, usually mounted on a postcard-sized piece of card.

- Postcard pictures (1906–1940s) can be recognized by their back, which is printed as a postcard.

- Autograph pictures (1914–1930s) is the name given to the technique of writing a message or reference number direct on to a negative. The 'Vest-Pocket Kodak' made this possible, and the instant success of this camera means that the feature is very common through the First World War and the 1920s.

- Tinted pictures (1890s–1950s) are a hybrid of photography and painting. While in theory as early as paper photography, there seem to be few early examples. The results are frequently disappointing; occasionally a true work of art is produced.

- Outdoor photographs (much more common from 1914) enabled large groups to be photographed together. The First World War is documented by many photographs of military units. In the postwar years large wedding parties are more frequently photographed out of doors, usually formally ordered and posed much as a military unit would be.

- Informal photographs (from the 1920s) belong to an age when amateurs could afford a camera. Typically such photographs still have a degree of staging. This is the period from which photographs of children become commonplace. Locations are frequently the home of the person photographed. Dogs and other pets may be included in the picture. Sports photographs with the participants in their sports clothes are rare before the 1920s.

- Candid photographs (from the 1950s) reflect faster exposure times and cheaper cameras, film and developing. Often the technical quality of these images is poor.

■ Colour photography was rare before the Second World War and infrequent until the early 1960s. That said, the technology for some form of colour photography existed as early as the late Victorian age, while in the 1920s photographic pioneer William Friese-Greene even managed to produce colour films of a high quality. But colour photography was surprisingly slow in becoming commonplace. The vast majority of Second World War photographs are black and white, and this remained the standard for formal photography until well into the 1960s. Unless you are very lucky indeed you will not find colour photographs of ancestors prior to the Second World War. Instead there was much early hand colouring of photos, with the better artists giving very pleasing results. The transition to mass colour photography is around 1970; by the early 1970s colour had all but replaced black and white save for specialist and art photography.

Dating the costume

For the non-specialist the easiest method of dating a costume is to find comparable costumes on dated photographs. Women's costumes show remarkably rapid variation and can usually be dated to a period of a decade or less. Men's costumes have been less subject to change.

Inevitably the area is one where a specialist in costume will have skills that the amateur does not – and the amateur will wish to proceed with care. But there are some giveaways. For example, in women's fashion the puffed 'leg-of-mutton' sleeves are character-istic of the 1890s and rare before or after. Tubular skirts – long and narrow, nicknamed 'hobble skirts' as the extreme expression of this fashion impeded a woman's walking – are characteristic of the years just before the First World War, typically 1910–14, and most unusual in any other period. For men, beards were a fashion of the years following the Crimean War, becoming most common in the 1860s before receding sharply in popularity. Men almost always wore lace-up boots (even with their Sunday best and on formal occasions) until the end of the 1920s when shoes took over.

Costumes were frequently provided by the photographic studio and may not therefore be the clothes of the sitter. There was a photographic fashion for Highland dress (throughout the UK) so the ancestor who appears in a kilt may have had no connection with Scotland whatsoever. Uniforms were sometimes photographic props, and sometimes even tunic and headgear may be from different regiments.

Figure 17 This 1926 photograph has several dating clues. The photographer's serial number on the deckchair (right) is characteristic of the 1920s, while men's boots (as here) were mostly replaced by shoes in the 1930s. The custom of wearing Sunday Best on the beach declined during the interwar years.

Dating the event

Throughout the nineteenth century a photograph usually required a decision to make a trip to the photographer's studio and, as a consequence, the vast majority of photographs from this period are associated with an event.

- Marriage photographs from the Victorian age often go unnoticed in albums. The white wedding dress that we now associate with a wedding was not then usual. Rather, the couple appear in their Sunday best. Indications that the photograph represents a wedding include a conspicuously displayed ring on the woman's hand and large floral button-holes. Some of the earliest wedding photographs are separate pictures of the bride and groom. Family group photographs are infrequent. Rather, other family members – for example, the parents, brothers and sisters of the married couple – might accompany the bride and groom to the studio and have their individual photographs taken at the same time.

- Completion of apprenticeship photos frequently display the tools of the trade.

- Funerals prompted photographs of the mourners, a custom now largely lost. Post-mortem pictures (photographs of the deceased) are sometimes to be found, though this custom was more common in America than in the British Isles.

- Sports teams that won an event often had photographs taken – but usually wearing their Sunday best, not their sports clothes. Photographs of groups of young men are frequently of sports teams.

Photographs commemorating events may be taken some time after the event. There are photographs extant of the 1840 wedding of Queen Victoria and Prince Albert. The bride and groom are in their wedding clothes – but the photographs were taken in 1854. Though the Daguerreotype was commercially available in London in 1840 it clearly did not occur to the courtiers organizing the wedding that a photograph might be appropriate – an oversight remedied fourteen years later.

IDEA

The National Archives
Examine the UK History Photo Finder from the National Archives at labs.nationalarchives.gov.uk – a growing resource around a nucleus of 14,000 pictures in the Dixon–Scott collection from 1926 to 1948.

IDEA

Video clips
Video clips are frequently made available through local studies centres in libraries. They are available from the 1890s (in theory even earlier) and in some number from around 1910. They tend to be of major public events and therefore show something your ancestor may have seen.

IDEA

Negatives
Sometimes it is negatives rather than prints that have been preserved. An easy way to 'develop' them is to scan them, then select 'negative' in image-editing software (creating a positive). This at least makes possible a decision on whether the negative is worth laboratory developing.

Many photographic prints fade over the years either through light exposure or simply through ageing. Negatives can provide images free from these problems.

27

Early genealogy

The British Isles as a whole, and England in particular, have been subject to an almost obsessive documentation from the High Middle Ages onwards. Amazingly, records do exist which enable some families to be traced from just a few generations after the Norman Conquest onwards. These oldest documents are available mostly through the PRO or CROs.

The enormous problem with such records is that they are almost all un-indexed, un-transcribed and un-translated, and they were not designed with a view to tracing families. Problems in using them are significant – for example, they are almost all ordered by place rather than by name. A degree of skill is needed in reading the records: the handwriting is challenging, and most are in Latin rather than English (and some of the very earlier records in Norman French). Making use of such records to trace a family is neither quick nor easy. Notwithstanding the challenge of using them, they are within the reach of keen genealogists.

Scotland

Scotland has a remarkable resource for mediaeval Scottish genealogy in the form of a comprehensive database of all people named in the charters of 1093–1286 (the death of Malcolm III to the death of Alexander III). If you can get back to this period – and some Scottish lines can be traced this far back, in contrast with most in England – then you may hit the jackpot. The website has the quirky name the Paradox of Medieval Scotland (www.poms. ac.uk), a reference to questions of Scottish ethnicity and identity which the site aims to address through an examination of the identities and relationships of some 6,000 names.

DEALING WITH LATIN

Latin was the legal language of the UK until 1733. For the genealogist researching lines prior to this date – and sometimes even subsequently – texts in Latin will be encountered: wills, deeds, manorial records, court rolls and much more. Early inscriptions in churches are frequently in Latin.

Dealing with the Latin of old documents was once a challenge which only the specialist could tackle. Some level of knowledge of Latin was once all but indispensable, and even those trained in the Classical Latin of Cicero would find the Anglo-Latin documents of the British Isles difficult.

FINDING SOLUTIONS

If you have some knowledge of Latin, however small, or even if you have familiarity with other languages and are ready to try your hand at a Latin document, then there is no reason why you should not succeed given sufficient time. However, translating even the shortest Latin document can take considerable time. Essential reading is Charles Trice Martin's *The Record Interpreter* (1892; reprinted 1999), which is still the standard work on the Latin of British mediaeval documents. This includes an extensive glossary of British Isles Latin, as well as listings of the very many contractions used.

Google Translation has come to the rescue with online translation from Latin to English. Simply type in the text you want translated and the software provides an English version. Purists will of course point out the shortcomings, and indeed there are very many, but (speaking as a mediaeval linguist) I venture the view that the software is superb as a starting point for anyone who is not a Latin specialist.

SOLVING A LATIN PUZZLE

The following inscription from Lydd Church (in Kent) is typical of the sort of Latin that may confront the genealogist. The actual carving is sharp so there really isn't much doubt about what is inscribed – but making sense of it is a different matter altogether:

> Arctus ad Coelos aditus: Decora
> Arctior multo latet ipsa Porta.
> Solus hae Altam repit in Quietem.

> Lacteus Infans.
> Robertas, Primogenitus Richardi Godfrey Gen', natus xi Aug. hinc demigrans xxvii°.
> Octo. proximo sequentis.

Google Translate does provide a starting point, though the translation it gives really needs improving, benefiting from some knowledge of Latin, however basic. A reasonable translation would be something like:

> Narrow is the approach to the Heavens: much narrower
> The proper gate itself lies hidden.
> The happy child alone crawls into the high rest.

An unweaned child.
Robert, first born of Richard Godfrey, gentleman, born 11th August, departed from here shortly afterwards the 27th October following.

This text is not easy even for a Latin specialist, not least because the Latin written in the British Isles had many conventions that differed from the Latin the Romans used. This is bad Classical Latin, though perfectly good British Isles Latin. The verse may have been written specifically for the inscription and, while I'm reasonably confident that the translation is correct, I'm not clear as to why this sentiment was considered appropriate.

IDEA

Ask for Latin help
The Internet has come to the help with the Latin Discussion Forum (www.latindiscussionforum.com) on which there is a section to 'Ask or give help with any Latin to English translations'. There may well be a kind soul who will do your translation for you! You are more likely to get help with short translations and you do need to interest someone in offering a translation, so you need to contextualize the Latin within family or local history.

COPING WITH HANDWRITING

The vast majority of the material we read today is printed. None of us gets much practice at reading handwriting. Reading old handwriting in order to decipher genealogical documents has always been a challenge, and it is one that is getting bigger.

British Isles handwriting styles

The quality and style of handwriting of documents in the British Isles have changed extensively through the centuries.

Curiously, some of our earliest records (those in Anglo-Saxon and Latin from the Early Middle Ages) are among the most legible, as 'joined-up' writing was not used and it is reasonably simple to decipher each individual letter.

The High Middle Ages produced secretary hand, a style of 'joined-up' writing which was often written at speed and which presents numerous difficulties. It has a level of illegibility which frequently baffles even the experts. Additionally many of the documents are in Latin, so the researcher is struggling both with the handwriting and the language. Family tree lines can go back this far, but the area is at the boundaries of that which can reasonably be studied by the amateur. Either specialist training or help from a hand-writing professional – or both – is needed.

The problem areas most often tackled by the genealogist are the sixteenth, seventeenth and eighteenth centuries. This is certainly challenging as the handwriting style is not familiar today but, none the less, can reasonably be tackled by the keen amateur.

Much writing from the nineteenth and twentieth century bears the hallmark of schoolroom teaching and can often be read with few difficulties. The handwriting from this period that is likely to be problematic for the genealogist is that which is quick or careless. This is frequently encountered in such documents as Victorian census schedules and First World War medal cards.

IDEA

Learn palaeography on the job
There are a handful of key ideas which help with any document.

▶ Write out an alphabet of letter forms as they appear in the document. A single letter may have several different forms.

▶ Remember that u/v and y/i/j were often treated as the same letter.

▶ Many documents contain set phrases as, for example, in the introduction to wills. If you cannot read your document, try another in the same archive.

▶ Spelling is frequently phonetic – do not expect words to conform to the dictionary spelling.

▶ Much use is made of abbreviations. Accent marks usually indicate letters which have been left off.

IDEA

Learning basic palaeography
Some skills can be learnt quickly and easily. A teach-yourself course has been created by the National Archives at www.nationalarchives.gov.uk/palaeography.

28

Genetics and genealogy

DNA studies are the exciting, new frontier of genealogical study. There are certainly occasions when a personal test can provide useful results. However, there are very severe limitations also. Despite the media and magazine hype around 'scientific' genealogy, it is so far no more than one tool, and often a very poor one at that.

BEWARE OF DNA GENEALOGY

First the bad news. In 2008, *Which? Computing* magazine sent the same set of DNA samples to four leading companies offering genealogists' DNA tests (including the two big ones), requesting the same tests. They found that results varied wildly. One of their editors, Sarah Kidner, commented that 'people need to be wary of DNA testing services...the results are so vague it's almost the equivalent of telling someone what their star sign is'.

Then the worse news. There have been doubts expressed about the security of the DNA material submitted to testing companies. It is far from clear whether these doubts have any real substance to them (the doubts are expressed in newspaper and magazine articles and online, and all seemingly without a reference to a specific incident that has raised the concerns). We have smoke without an identified fire, but our culture tells us there is no smoke without fire. Some companies may have excellent security – some may not. The small print might say that your DNA is stored for twenty years. It might say that your DNA is shared with other similar companies, which sounds as if it means with other genealogists' DNA testing services but may also mean with pharmaceutical companies. I don't know how anyone can be confident that there is no possibility whatsoever of stored DNA results being leaked or shared with companies you may not wish to access them.

A bit more bad news is that a test costs from around £100 to around £500 – and the cheaper ones are probably not worth considering as the information they yield is too vague. Ethnic origin tests can be even more expensive.

UNDERSTANDING THE THEORY

The way forward with a DNA test is to understand what can and cannot be done. If you select the right company and the right test you can (in some circumstances) gain results useful for family-tree study. The area has enormous potential, but right now that potential is often not realized. The potential does include that of breaking down those brick walls where written records utterly fail.

For the genealogist there are three types of tests to consider.

■ Mitochondrial DNA: this is passed from mother to children, and women and men can both have this test. The area has developed because of the realization that human populations at an early stage in our development passed through a set of genetic bottlenecks, a consequence of which is that (for example) all Europeans are descended from just seven or so women (and presumably a similarly small number of men, though the test has nothing to say about these). These women – nicknamed 'the daughters of Eve' – are associated with different locations. A mitochondrial DNA test identifies the specific daughter of Eve from whom you are descended in the female line. It therefore says something about a very, very distant female-line ancestor and suggests where she might have lived. Of course this goes well beyond genealogy. It also sidesteps the reality that every one in Europe is descended by one line or another from all seven of the European daughters of Eve.

■ Tests around ethnic origin are so far the least used in genealogy. This is because they are expensive. The underlying concept is that particular genetic markers can be identified as characteristic of a particular ethnicity, and the mix within an individual's genetic make-up can be identified in percentage terms. However, it is not as simple as having a test and being checked against all races in the world – rather, testing is by checking an individual's DNA sample against a list of ethnic types – and generally this is a short list. If you suspect that your British Isles ancestry contains (say) a great-grandparent from a different ethnic group it would in theory be possible to check specifically for this. But most commercial services don't offer this sort of check.

■ Y-chromosome DNA testing examines the male Y-chromosome – so only men can have this test. This is the most useful test for genealogists as Y-chromosome transmission corresponds with surname transmission, and a Y-chromosome test works well alongside a one-name surname study. The 'monogenetic revolution' is the realization that all but our most common surnames had a single first bearer, and that people with the same surname are usually related. It is practical for men who share the same surname to prove their kinship using a Y-chromosome DNA test. Where surnames are bi-genetic (had two points of origin) or a small number of points of origin it is possible to prove connection with a specific group. Most of the testing companies seek to use their own databases to link people who take a Y-chromosome test with their relatives. However, the most useful results are obtained when the test is alongside a one-surname study.

THE DNA OF THE BRITISH ISLES

We used to think we knew all about the ethnic make-up of the British Isles. We used to think that the population of the British Isles were in ethnic terms a mix of English and Celtic, with the English dominant in most of England and the Celts in Wales, Scotland and Ireland. Add a sprinkle of Viking and Norman French, and that was pretty much the mix that we thought made up the British. Now we know for certain that we were wrong – yet this discredited and untenable old view still influences how people think about their ethnicity.

Today we know that a 'typical' British Isles profile (from anywhere in the British Isles) will be made up mainly of two ethnic groups. One, the most common, is usually called 'Celtic', though it predates the arrival of the Celtic languages and people in the British Isles (and should therefore be called pre-Celtic, though the term hasn't caught on). The other is Germanic, and is the genetic profile of both the Anglo-Saxons and their cousins the Vikings. For the most part it has not been possible to tell apart the Anglo-Saxons and the Vikings. The indigenous people of the British Isles all show a mix of these two groups, with typically twice as much 'Celtic' as Germanic. If your ancestry is British Isles your DNA mix is pretty much two thirds 'Celtic' and one third Anglo-Saxon and Viking combined.

Norman French really doesn't get a look in, partly because there weren't many Normans who came to Britain and partly because their genetic mix was only part French – remember the Norman French were themselves of Viking origin, which is why they are called Norsemen or Normans. For that matter, true Celtic genes, those of the Celts who inhabited central Europe, are almost never found in the British Isles. The arrival of the Celts into the British Isles was an arrival of language and culture, not of people. The people we call Celts have Celtic language and culture but not a continental Celtic ethnicity – rather their ethnicity is pre-Celtic, what you might like to think of as the people who built Stonehenge.

So two thirds 'Celtic' and one third Anglo-Saxon and Viking (Germanic) is the basic mix for the indigenous population of the British Isles. There are variations: the Germanic DNA proportion is a bit more than a third in eastern England, while the 'Celtic' DNA proportion is a bit more than two thirds in England's West Country, in Wales and in Ireland. However, the overwhelming picture is of genetic conformity throughout the British Isles. That said there are some truly amazing surprises. For example, the people of Scotland have the same qualities of 'Celtic' DNA as the people of Kent, indicating that the Scots are as English as the people of Kent, or the people of Kent as Scottish as the Scots. No one would have predicted this, and quite a few people are upset by such findings.

The British indigenous population clearly shows more ethnicities than just 'Celtic' and Germanic. Jewish, French, Mediterranean and Romany genes can be distinguished (if appropriate tests are carried out). Most controversial are claims to Norwegian Viking genes. There is a theory that a genetic profile for Norwegian Vikings has been identified. Certainly there is a distinctive genetic profile which exists in many areas we believe the Norwegian Vikings settled, but it is a jump to say that this is a Norwegian Viking genetic profile. All the Vikings – Danish and Norwegian and others – believed themselves to be one people and spoke the same language, and we know they inter-married extensively. It is most likely that Norwegian Vikings would have substantially the same genetic profile as the Danish Vikings – and therefore the same as Anglo-Saxons. Of course this begs the question as to quite what the genetic marker that has been found and identified as Norwegian Viking might be. Just possibly it is Pictish.

EMPLOYING DNA IN ONE-NAME STUDIES

Assuming marriage and legitimacy, 100% of a man's children bear his surname. As surname transmission is comparable with Y-chromosome transmission it makes sense to link a Y-chromosome study with a one-name study.

The overwhelming advantage of one-name studies is the simplicity of the concept. It bundles together all records relating to one surname and draws together the patrilineal connections. The ideal is often the establishment of an ultimate ancestor from whom all bearers of the surname can be traced, and this is indeed sometimes possible. DNA analysis offers a tool to prove the line established by the records.

The disadvantage is how few of a man's descendants are picked up by a one-name study. It is worth bearing in mind from the outset just how limiting this can be. Because of the practice of women taking their husband's surname, only 50% of the first surname bearer's grandchildren (as an average) and 25% of his great-grandchildren will be born with his surname (and of these many will subsequently change it through marriage). After five generations, only just over 3% of a man's descendants will bear his surname, while after ten generations the number is less than 1%. Ten generations – 300 years or thereabouts – might take you back to the late seventeenth century, well within reach of genealogical research. A one-name study is going to include less than 1% of descendants alive today – and leave out more than 99%.

Realistically you may wish to be involved in many surname studies, not just those that relate to your own surname. Yet you can only make a direct Y-chromosome DNA contribution to the study which relates to your surname.

IDEA

The daughters of Eve

You can explore your mitochondrial DNA without actually having a test done. The 'daughters of Eve' are the subject of countless articles in print and online. The original concept is found in the book by Bryan Sykes, *The Seven Daughters of Eve* (W.W. Norton, 2001). If you are European you are descended by one route or another from all seven. Work by Sykes and others has suggested that the whole of the world's population is descended from about three-dozen daughters of Eve. All these three dozen women ultimately share a common maternal ancestor, the so-called 'mitochondrial Eve'. Genetics appears to have proved the Eve of *Genesis* – and reminded us that we are all related.

What a mitochondrial DNA test can do is tell you who among the daughters of Eve is your specific mother's mother's mother's mother's... Sykes has given these seven women names (Ursula, Xenia, Helena, Velda, Tara, Katrine and Jasmine) and has suggested the time, location and lifestyle of each. A test might give you a sense of personal link to one of these.

IDEA

DNA test
If you do decide to go ahead with a DNA test:

▶ use a major company (unless you are part of a one-surname study that is using a specific smaller company);

▶ satisfy yourself that your DNA record will be appropriately secured – or decide that you don't object should it be leaked;

▶ decide exactly which test you want and what you hope to learn;

▶ note that the cheaper 'entry level' DNA tests are of very little use; and

▶ order your testing kit. The practicality of a genealogy DNA test is that a self-administered cheek-swab is used.

IDEA

Wait
Consider postponing your DNA test. I have no doubt that DNA genealogy will in the future be standard. But we're not there yet. DNA sequencing is getting much cheaper, which will assist development – and concerns around security and accuracy will presumably be resolved.

29

Heritage

We long to belong. Of people who live away from the place where they grew up and where they have family, over half report that they would like to move back. But the sense of yearning for roots goes much deeper. The same 2008 survey (by Opinium Research for FindMyPast.com) found that one person in ten in the British Isles today would like to move to the home of distant ancestors, even if they had never visited this location.

We want to know our roots, but we also want to know the heritage that goes with those roots. A focus on heritage rather than a family line may help to circumvent some genealogy brick walls. You may not be able to trace a particular line in which you are interested back through the generations but you may be able to localize your ancestors within an area and a culture and understand more of this culture.

One extreme is that the indigenous people of the British Isles have been shown by DNA studies to be very closely inter-related – quite literally everyone of British origins is related to everyone else, with common ancestors no more than seven centuries ago, a blink of an eye in the timeline of genetics. We are all related to the royal line of Prince William and all related to the commoners of Kate Middleton's ancestry.

In genetic terms the kinship is with the whole British Isles more than with any one home nation or area. Yet, for many, concepts such as English, Welsh, Scottish and Irish are meaningful.

Certificate your Irish cultural heritage

Most British Isles family lines have an Irish connection somewhere – indeed if you don't know of one it is probably only because you haven't found it yet. We are indeed (almost) all a little bit Irish, and not just on St Patrick's Day.

Today round seven million people live in the island of Ireland, both in Northern Ireland and the Republic of Ireland. The Republic of Ireland is renowned for a concept of citizenship more liberal than most nations. In addition to offering Irish passports to UK citizens of Northern Ireland, the so-called 'granny rule' means that the children and grandchildren of any native-born Irish person (born anywhere in the island of Ireland) have the right of full citizenship. If you have a grandparent born in Ireland then your heritage is the right to an Irish passport.

Recently the government of the Republic of Ireland has looked at the Irish diaspora and concluded that there are around seventy million people of Irish descent living around the world, most with more distant connections with Ireland than those captured by the 'granny rule'. Those not eligible for an Irish passport will be eligible (from 2012, subject to franchising negotiations) for a state-issued document from the Department of Foreign Affairs called a 'Certificate of Irish Heritage'. This confers 'official Irishness' on people who have a sense of affinity with Ireland. It is a serious idea by which the nation state of Ireland plans to keep in touch with the overseas Irish community by an acknowledgement of heritage.

IDEA

Tartan and Scotland

Tartan is as old as weaving. It was traditional throughout Scotland, as well as in the north of England and in Ireland. There was a loose association of patterns with areas, families and regiments, though the idea of a unique family tartan is almost entirely a nineteenth-century invention. The fashion can be traced to the 1822 visit of King George IV to Edinburgh. As part of the pageantry many of the Scottish dignitaries wished to appear in their 'ancestral' tartan, prompting the first wholesale creation of tartans. The Victorian age continued the process so that, by the end of the nineteenth century, just about every Scottish surname had its tartan. Tartans are still being created today.

Tartan designs are not ancient, and you can be sure that a Scottish ancestor who fought at Culloden (1745) would not have been wearing the tartan today associated with his surname. Yet the nineteenth and twentieth centuries have promoted the idea that someone with a particular surname is 'entitled' to a particular tartan. People who share the same Scottish surname probably are related, so in effect the tartan is being used as a modern uniform to stress a distant kinship. The clans, mostly twentieth-century revivals, stress a shared heritage and reflect this with a shared tartan. Tartan can express Scottish heritage and a sense of belonging to a particular extended family – or it can simply be an international fashion statement, as familiar in Tokyo as New York.

If you have Scottish roots, find out what tartan is associated with your surname. If you have an ancestor who served in a Scottish regiment, find out what tartan they would have worn. Tartan can be an outward sign of heritage.

IDEA

Wales and Welsh

Today only a minority of the people of Wales use the Welsh language on a day-to-day basis, yet just a couple of centuries ago almost everyone in

Wales was Welsh speaking. If your family is from Wales then your ancestors were Welsh speakers.

In the UK more resource is put into teaching Welsh than into any language other than English. Welsh is the learnt language showing the fastest growth. People want to learn Welsh. The motivation is rarely for practical necessity but rather because people identify with Welsh culture. If your heritage is Welsh consider learning the language. It will help no end with your genealogical research through parish registers written in Welsh, but most of all it will make you feel closer to your Welsh-speaking ancestors.

30

Cost-benefit analysis for research

Genealogy is not intrinsically an expensive hobby, and much can be done for free. However, when tackling a brick wall, costs can add up quickly. It makes sense to start with the free and cheap resources, and make targeted use of the more expensive ones.

Many records are available from only one source and, if you want to see the record, you have no alternative but to purchase the copy. One of the most expensive areas can be those records which ask for a voluntary donation for access, as you may feel obliged to donate pounds for the sort of information ordinarily available online for pennies. If you regard this as a charge for access it is often astronomic; if you are happy to donate to the charity set out you may regard the access as free.

The key issue before buying genealogical services is whether you are sure of learning something from the record you are buying.

USING FREE RESOURCES

The free resource in every community is the public library. Free, online access to databases supported by the public library system is a remarkable resource – and well worth investigating. The public libraries can obtain books through the Inter-library Loan system, so access to specialist printed sources is available from even the most modest public library. There is a small administrative charge for Inter-library Loans.

Use free online sources where they are available. An excellent example is FreeBMD (www.freebmd.org.uk), which is a transcription of the Civil Registration index for England and Wales. The system is funded by banner advertisements and donations, with the indexes transcribed by volunteers. The transcription is not yet comprehensive. Work has started with the earliest records (1837) and has now reached the 1950s, so the majority of records of interest to genealogists are available.

FreeBMD has a couple of features not found in the original indexes. It has a postem system which allows users to post information of what they believe to be mistakes, which may serve as a shortcut to finding information which has been erroneously entered or transcribed. It also has a workaround for finding the names of a spouse from the marriage index. The original index lists the surname of the spouse only from 1912, so before this date you need to know the name of both bride and groom to look up an entry. However, FreeBMD gives the district, volume and page number of a marriage, then allows you to search for other entries on this same page. Typically a page contains two marriages (some, however, contain four) so you can access the names of two brides and two grooms, without knowing who married whom. Often a search in the census which followed the marriage reveals the couple and provides an answer. FreeBMD also provides scans of the original index so that you can check transcription.

GOOD VALUE FROM ONLINE SUBSCRIPTION SERVICES

There are dozens of subscription genealogy services. At present the two biggest are Ancestry and FindMyPast. While both offer some records for free, both require a subscription for full access. These and other subscription services have a variety of packages and discounts, but typically work out in the region of just over £100 p.a. subscription. If you are a heavy user of genealogy records they are excellent value for money. It is worth exploring special offers, which might include free trial membership or promotional prices. Some online subscription services discriminate between completely new customers and those who have previously used their free services – the former getting the cheaper price. Presumably the thinking is that just about anyone who joins will do so through a special offer, and this is only being granted once. Many sites split their records by region, with subscribers requiring records worldwide paying more than those who require just British Isles records.

The keenest genealogists might subscribe to both Ancestry and FindMyPast – and to many of the others. Most genealogists appear to select one or the other – and there is no easy answer to the question of which is better. Indeed they are well matched, and there is significant overlap. It makes sense to look at the detail of what each offers and make a decision on that basis. For example, the London parish registers from the London Metropolitan Archive are (at the time of writing) available only from Ancestry and may persuade a genealogist with London ancestors to use this site. However (at the time of writing) FindMyPast has the only online access to the Society of Genealogists' collections.

Remember that the site Ancestry is available for free through the UK public library system – and it is its worldwide coverage that is free, not just the British Isles records. This does not seem well advertised and many keen genealogists are unaware of it, but you can get all the search services of this website for free if you sit at a public terminal in the library. There are a few libraries not covered as the decision to provide a database is taken by each library area, but these exceptions do seem very rare. There may also be restrictions on uploading family trees and viewing existing family trees, but these may be minor inconveniences for free access. Public library access to Ancestry may be either a way of checking out their collections prior to subscribing, or may be an alternative to subscription.

REGRETTING **BMD** COSTS

Some of the highest costs are generated by obtaining birth, marriage and death certificates. The rationale is that these documents are legal documents – i.e. they are certificates. At the time of writing costs are £10 in England and Wales, £10 in Scotland and £14 in Northern Ireland. There are around 2,000 BMD certificates that I would like to see, but £20,000 is an unthinkable expense.

Efforts to circumvent the charges by requesting access to individual certificates under freedom-of-information legislation have failed because the current fee system is deemed to provide reasonable access.

In theory legislation is in place to provide a proper index. In practice there seems to be little progress. Meanwhile a 'check' service – whereby for a reduced fee an official would check specific details on a certificate assisting in finding the right one – has been withdrawn.

NOTICE BOARDS

The online forum is a wonder of the Internet. This is where we can all get help from experts. Usually it is as simple as asking – and it's free.

It is crucial that requests for help are presented clearly.

- Titles of postings should include full names, places, dates.

- Full names, including maiden names, should be used throughout.

- Dates should be given where known, and approximate dates where they are not.

- The distinction between fact and speculation should be clear.

- You should share your information.

- Be clear what information you are seeking.

IDEA

Free records
Consider the following when using free records.

▶ Make full use of free records: online and through public libraries. Use trial subscriptions to services and avoid duplication of access through subscription to two or more similar services.

▶ Working with fellow researchers may allow you to split costs. This is particularly the case with BMD certificates.

▶ Use substitutes which are cheap or free instead of records you have to pay for. For example, church records of christenings, marriages and burials provide most of the information that you would find on a BMD certificate and access may well be free. The 1881 census is available for free – use this in preference to 1871 or 1891.

IDEA

Consider genealogy ebooks and ejournals
Some titles are available for free on your computer; others are available through public and university libraries. For example, the online Oxford Reference Collection includes the *Oxford Dictionary of Local and Family History* (Oxford University Press, 2001), a useful dictionary of genealogical terms.

Some of the major ejournals for the British Isles are:

▶ *Annals of Genealogical Research*;

▶ *Family and Community History* ;

▶ *The History of the Family*;

▶ *Journal of Family History*.

31

The genealogy industry

Genealogy has come of age. It has even attracted a set of commemorative stamps in the form of a set of eight from the Isle of Man issued on 18 February 2011. But most of all it has become so large that it has become an industry, transcending the world of the hobbyist and the antiquarian.

Figure 18 *Who Do You Think You Are? Live!* – the biggest genealogy meeting in the British Isles, at Earls Court.

A glimpse at the size of the new industry is given by the *Who Do You Think You Are? LIVE!* show at London's Olympia conference hall. The show started in 2007 and in that year attracted 7,500 visitors. By 2011 the number was up to 11,000, and there is every expectation of increase in each of the next few years. The format is that visitors attend workshops and tour the stands of the various genealogy companies and learned societies looking for solutions to their family-tree brick walls. But only a tiny fraction of British Isles genealogists actually visit this show – perhaps one in a hundred. The number of people in the British Isles with a hobby in genealogy is perhaps in excess of a million. This huge number represents a commercial opportunity for a new and growing industry.

LOOKING TO THE FUTURE

The future for genealogy is bright mainly because of the investment that is being generated by this new industry. The developments that we can expect soon include the following.

■ Even cheaper access to all census records – in addition to the free 1881 census. Very many amateurs are transcribing and making available the records for their local area, and this process is eroding the ability of the subscription services to charge for access.

■ Free or much cheaper access to BMD records comparable with the access available to the census. In theory legislation is in place for this to happen – in practice it is taking a very long time to implement. Right now we have the disgrace that these key, public documents for history are behind an excessive pay barrier – but there will be a solution.

■ Better indexing of military records. The First World War medal cards have whet the appetite of genealogists for online military records. The commercial digitization of earlier records will come in time.

■ Countless small archives are coming online or otherwise becoming accessible. In part this is because of freedom-of-information legislation, in part because companies are prepared to undertake the work.

■ Memorial inscriptions: this is an area where amateur contributions are still the key. Increasingly we are seeing communities create and expand their websites, providing a space for documents such as these to be published.

■ Electoral rolls: digitization is the key here, turning a source which has been difficult to access and frustratingly slow to research into something which can be accessed in seconds.

■ Printed books: the drive is to digitize books so that obscure, old volumes can be accessed through the Internet. In addition to easier access, digitization provides easier searching, so a single mention of an ancestor's name within a volume can now be picked up by a search engine.

■ Newspapers: so far we have scarcely scratched the surface of the digitization of newspapers, yet already this is proving to be a rich source for the genealogist. Much more is to be expected, and soon.

■ Oral histories: collections are being made and indexed, and it may well be that in the future these will be seen as a key resource.

- Overseas records: nowhere is as privileged as the British Isles with availability of and access to genealogical records, but others are catching up.

- DNA: this exciting area surely offers the most future promise.

IDEA

Consider a course
Genealogy is now supported by many courses. If you want to tackle brick walls these might be a good way forward.

▶ Local courses are frequently offered by local authorities, libraries and family history societies. They usually offer the chance to talk with other genealogists. If your ancestry is from the area in which you now live, these courses are particularly appropriate as there is usually a focus on local records.

▶ Many universities are now offering genealogy courses. These are sometimes extra-mural (i.e. leading to no formal qualification) though increasingly they offer a certificate or diploma. Some are by distance learning.

▶ Courses are also available in local history, a discipline which utilizes many of the skills required for family history. Typically such courses include materials on the methodology for approaching historical evidence and are increasingly dominated by the creation and use of databases of material – indeed the quantitative element of some courses is so great that they can be studied as an MSc qualification. Most courses seem to target the amateurs keen on researching the history of their local area. They offer concepts and methodology for approaching local history, taking it out of the traditional realm of antiquarian study and into the rigorous academic discipline of historical research. Many focus on the creation and use of databases in order to question, manipulate and analyse data.

Appendix – The top 10 brick wall tips

1. Something isn't right – so check your facts
Common mistakes include the following.

- You have made a transcription error, or otherwise got your facts wrong.

- You have believed a family story which isn't supported by the records.

- A relative has thought about a family story, interpreted it in the light of their knowledge of history, and produced a garbled version.

- More than one person shares your ancestor's name.

Solution tip: write out the key facts about an ancestor's life along with the sources.

2. The person you are looking for just can't be found
Solution tip: consider name variants.

3. You have searched a database but not found what you are looking for
Solution tip: improve your search criteria for interrogating the database. Remember that the database is an index and may contain mistakes. Where possible look at the original records.

4. Your line just won't go back
Solution tip: go sideways. Search collateral lines.

5. Your line won't go backwards or sideways
Solution tip: try cluster genealogy – search for records relating to the whole community.

6. You have run out of ideas
Solution tip: make full use of online boards.

7. You are stuck, absolutely and completely stuck
Solution tip: try jumping the block. Look at possible ancestors further back and see if you can find reference to their descendants as a way to link them to your ancestors.

8. Nothing is working
Solution tip: if you have checked thoroughly and checked again and still drawn a blank you need some new record source. Think outside the box – what other records are there?

9. Still nothing
Solution tip: consider sources of information about genealogical research. These include books (well done for reading this one!), magazines and courses. There's also a place for employing a specialist to look at complex records.

10. And still nothing.
Solution tip: just because there isn't a solution now doesn't mean that there won't be a solution in the future.

Index

SOME OTHER TITLES FROM HOW TO BOOKS

YOUR FAMILY TREE ON-LINE
How to trace your ancestry from your own computer
DR GRAEME DAVIS

Graeme Davis's thorough guide is a step-by-step guide to using the wealth of on-line records to trace your family tree from your own computer without the need to travel to national and regional record offices. With this book you can make real progress, however little or much you already know about your family tree, whether you are a novice or an experienced genealogist, and whether you plan to devote just a few hours of time or embark on a life-time hobby.

This book guides you through the mass of records available: birth, marriage and death, the census, and much, much more – so that you can find out more about your family tree. There are records available from your computer that can take your line back hundreds of years, as well as sources that will help you connect with cousins living today. As you trace your line, this book will show you how to upload your results to the internet, both to preserve your family's heritage and to connect with relatives.

The focus throughout is on outcomes, on what you can actually achieve. However much or little time you have you can make progress with the help of this book. Whether it is investigating a family story, tracking down relatives, exchanging photos and reminiscences, or a simple curiosity to know more, this book will guide you.

ISBN 978-1-84528-344-5

RESEARCH YOUR SURNAME

and your family tree
DR GRAEME DAVIS

Find out what your surname means and trace your ancestors who share it too.

This comprehensive book will show you how to research your surname and your family tree, both in the earliest and in more recent years. It provides practical activities to investigate the meaning of any British surname. You will discover:

- The meaning of your surname;
- How old it is;
- Where it comes from;
- What associations it has today;
- How to use your surname to trace ancestors.

You may also be able to take part in a One Name Study or use DNA profiling to make contact with other people who bear your surname and with whom you share distant ancestors.

ISBN 978-1-84528-434-3

HOW TO TRACE YOUR IRISH ANCESTORS

An essential guide to researching and documenting the family histories of Ireland's people
IAN MAXWELL

'A solid account of Ireland's records written in a clear, accessible manner.' Who Do You Think You Are?

The purpose of this book is to highlight the most important documentary evidence available to the family historian wishing to research their Irish ancestry. It is aimed primarily at researchers whose time in Irish repositories is limited, and who want to know what is available locally and online. It covers more than 18 individual sources of information, making it simpler to organise your search and easier to carry it out both locally and on the ground.

ISBN 978-1-84528-375-9

WRITING YOUR LIFE STORY

How to record and present your memories for friends and family to enjoy
MICHAEL OKE

'Offers hundreds of ideas, memory joggers and techniques that will help the novice bring their story to life.' – Goodtimes Magazine

'It's often said that everyone has a book in them. A book offering tips on writing an autobiography was heard on Steve Wright's show. This was Michael Oke's *Writing Your Life Story*.' – Books in the Media

'Making a professional job of your autobiography is a very worthwhile project and *Writing Your Life Story* will help you make a polished job of it.' – Writing Magazine

ISBN 978-1-84528-399-5

THE JOY OF ENGLISH

100 illuminating conversations about the English language
JESSE KARJALAINEN

This is a pencil-sharp book about English for anyone who ever needs to write. In an easy-to-read style, it offers accessible and constructive advice to help you improve your English skills. It targets common pitfalls and those troublesome areas of English usage that affect everyone, no matter what their level of competence. It exposes several language myths and is bursting with 1500 examples of both right and wrong usage.

The Joy of English cuts to the heart of what readers want: help with their English. Its 100 short chapters are written in plain English and provide answers to the questions that we are too afraid to ask – amateurs and professionals alike.

Questions such as:

- Who *versus* whom
- Less *versus* fewer
- As *versus* because
- In contrast to *versus* by contrast
- Further *versus* farther
- Learned *versus* learnt
- Imply *versus* infer
- Practice *versus* practise
- Provided *versus* providing

We live in the information age. Never in history has the need to communicate been so great. We are writing, blogging and speaking more than ever before.

Everyone can improve their language skills, and enjoy their use of English as never before. The author boldly promises to change your English for ever, and put you on the path to new levels of competence and confidence.

ISBN 978-1-84528-478-7

How To Books are available through all good bookshops, or you can order direct from us through Grantham Book Services.

Tel: +44 (0)1476 541080
Fax: +44 (0)1476 541061
Email: Orders@gbs.tbs-ltd.co.uk

Or via our website www.howtobooks.co.uk

To order via any of these methods please quote the title(s) of the book(s) and your credit card number together with its expiry date.

For further information about our books and catalogue, please contact:

How To Books
Spring Hill House
Spring Hill Road
Begbroke
Oxford
OX5 1RX

Visit our web site at www.howtobooks.co.uk

Or you can contact us by email at info@howtobooks.co.uk